P9-CRD-057

KNAPP BRANCH LIBRARY
13330 CONANT
DETROIT, MICHIGAN 48212
(313) 852-4283

KN
DEC 10

Benjamin Banneker

George R. Carruthers

Shirley Ann Jackson

Ernest Everett Just

Walter E. Massey

John P. Moon

Daniel Hale Williams

Jane Cooke Wright

BRILLIANT
African-American
Scientists

9 Exceptional Lives

Charles R. Drew

Brilliant Doctor Who Made it
Possible to Store Donated Blood
for Longer Periods of Time.

MyReportLinks.com Books
an imprint of
Enslow Publishers, Inc. E
Box 398, 40 Industrial Road
Berkeley Heights, NJ 07922
USA

Jeff C. Young

To my sister, Stephanie Sue Walters

MyReportLinks.com Books, an imprint of Enslow Publishers, Inc. MyReportLinks®
is a registered trademark of Enslow Publishers, Inc.

Copyright © 2009 by Enslow Publishers, Inc.

All rights reserved.

No part of this book may be reproduced by any means
without the written permission of the publisher.

Library of Congress Cataloging-in-Publication Data

Young, Jeff C., 1948–
  Brilliant African-American scientists : nine exceptional lives / Jeff C. Young.
     p. cm. — (Great scientists and famous inventors)
  Summary: "Read about Benjamin Banneker, George R. Carruthers, Charles R.
Drew, Shirley Ann Jackson, Ernest Everett Just, Walter E. Massey, John P.
Moon, Daniel Hale Williams, and Jane Cooke Wright"--Provided by publisher.
  Includes bibliographical references and index.
  ISBN-13: 978-1-59845-083-5
  ISBN-10: 1-59845-083-2
  1. African American scientists—Biography—Juvenile literature. 2. Scientists—
United States—Biography—Juvenile literature. I. Title.
  Q141.Y674 2009
  509.2'273—dc22
  [B]
                            2008053924

032010 Lake Book Manufacturing, Inc., Melrose Park, IL

Printed in the United States of America

10 9 8 7 6 5 4 3 2

To Our Readers:
Through the purchase of this book, you and your library gain access to the Report Links that specifically back up this book. The Publisher will provide access to the Report Links that back up this book and will keep these Report Links up to date on **www.myreportlinks.com** for five years from the book's first publication date.
We have done our best to make sure all Internet addresses in this book were active and appropriate when we went to press. However, the author and the Publisher have no control over, and assume no liability for, the material available on those Internet sites or on other Web sites they may link to.
The usage of the MyReportLinks.com Books Web site is subject to the terms and conditions stated on the Usage Policy Statement on **www.myreportlinks.com**.
A password may be required to access the Report Links that back up this book. The password is found on the bottom of page 4 of this book.
Any comments or suggestions can be sent by e-mail to comments@myreportlinks.com or to the address on the back cover.

♻ Enslow Publishers, Inc., is committed to printing our books on recycled paper. The paper in every book contains 10% to 30% post-consumer waste (PCW). The cover board on the outside of each book contains 100% PCW. Our goal is to do our part to help young people and the environment too!

Photo Credits: African Scientific Institute/Shutterstock.com, p. 86; American Association for Cancer Research, p. 116; American Association for the Advancement of Science, pp. 63, 76; American Red Cross, p. 38; AP/Wide World Photos, pp. 56–57, 64, 78; Argonne National Laboratory, p. 74; Courtesy Rensselaer Polytechnic Institute, pp. 50, 60; Digital Stock Photos, p. 20; Dr. Scott Williams, p. 24; Five College Archives & Manuscript Collections, p. 112; Howard University, p. 43; HowStuffWorks, Inc., p. 91; IBM, p. 88; Library of Congress, pp. 13, 17, 105; Mark McCarty/American Association for the Advancement of Science, p. 61; Massachusetts Institute of Technology, pp. 30, 40; Mitchell C. Brown, pp. 5, 72; Morehouse College, p. 84; MyReportLinks.com Books, p. 4; NASA, pp. 22, 26, 28–29, 31; National Library of Medicine, pp. 96, 110, 115; Northwestern University, p. 99; Photo provided courtesy of the Naval Research Laboratory, p. 34; San Jose State University, p. 70; Schomburg Center for Research in Black Culture, the New York Public Library, Astor Lenox and Tilden Foundations, pp. 10, 102, 108; Shutterstock.com, pp. 8, 46, 52–53, 92; Smithsonian Institution, pp. 7, 32; Stanford University, p. 94; Teaching Pre K-8, p. 48; The Educational Broadcasting Corporation, p. 44; The Granger Collection, New York, pp. 1, 36, 69; The National Science Foundation, pp. 54, 81; The Provident Foundation, p. 101; Time Inc., pp. 18, 66; WGBH/PBS Online, pp. 14, 104.

Cover Photo: The Granger Collection, New York.

CONTENTS

About MyReportLinks.com Books..... 4

Introduction 5

1 **BENJAMIN BANNEKER** 10

2 **GEORGE R. CARRUTHERS** 22

3 **CHARLES R. DREW** 36

4 **SHIRLEY ANN JACKSON** 50

5 **ERNEST EVERETT JUST** 64

6 **WALTER E. MASSEY** 74

7 **JOHN P. MOON** 86

8 **DANIEL HALE WILLIAMS** 96

9 **JANE COOKE WRIGHT** 108

Report Links 118

Glossary 120

Chapter Notes 122

Further Reading............. 125

Index 126

MyReportLinks.com Books
Great Books, Great Links, Great for Research!

The Internet sites featured in this book can save you hours of research time. These Internet sites—we call them **"Report Links"**—are constantly changing, but we keep them up to date on our Web site.

When you see this "Approved Web Site" logo, you will know that we are directing you to a great Internet site that will help you with your research.

Give it a try! Type http://www.myreportlinks.com into your browser, click on the series title and enter the password, then click on the book title, and scroll down to the Report Links listed for this book.

The Report Links will bring you to great source documents, photographs, and illustrations. MyReportLinks.com Books save you time, feature Report Links that are kept up to date, and make report writing easier than ever! A complete listing of the Report Links can be found on pages 118–119 at the back of the book.

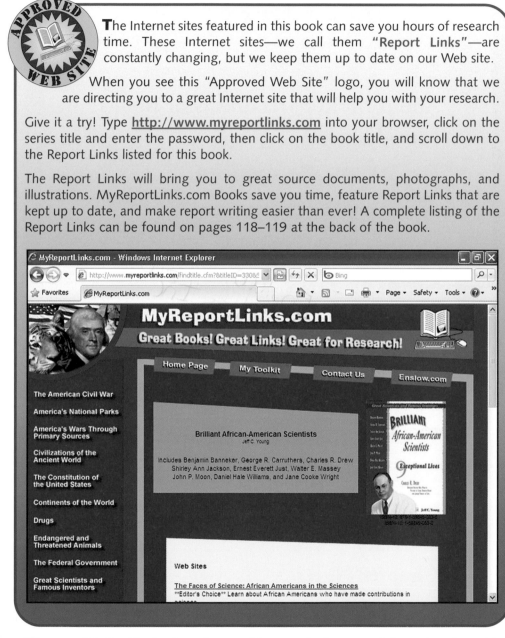

Please see "To Our Readers" on the copyright page for important information about this book, the MyReportLinks.com Web site, and the Report Links that back up this book.

Please enter **BAA1872** if asked for a password.

Introduction

The history of African-American involvement in American science goes back to the Colonial era (c.1500–1775). Free African Americans became known for their technical, scientific, and inventive skills. Benjamin Banneker was the first well-known African American to earn a national reputation for his scientific achievements. Banneker became a noted astronomer, mathematician, and publisher of almanacs in the late eighteenth and early nineteenth centuries.

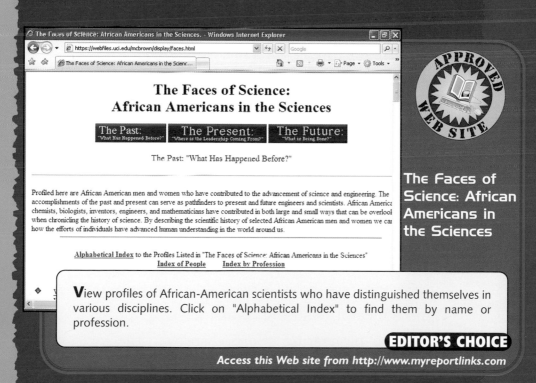

The Faces of Science: African Americans in the Sciences

View profiles of African-American scientists who have distinguished themselves in various disciplines. Click on "Alphabetical Index" to find them by name or profession.

EDITOR'S CHOICE

Access this Web site from http://www.myreportlinks.com

After the abolition of slavery in America in 1865, there was a gradual increase in the number of African Americans pursuing scientific careers. This growth was aided by the establishment of colleges and universities for African Americans. Yet, many of these schools offered only a few science courses. Their main emphasis was on preparing African Americans for careers as teachers, doctors, nurses, or clergymen.

African Americans wanting a thorough science education had to seek admission to white colleges and universities. Even when they could get the required education for a career as a scientist or researcher, racial discrimination kept them out of professional positions. In 1876, Edward Alexander Bouchet earned his PhD in physics from Yale University. But instead of working as a physicist, Bouchet had to take a job as a high school science teacher.

In twentieth-century America, there was a marked increase in African Americans entering the scientific field and making it their career. Some of the most notable were surgeon and blood researcher, Charles R. Drew; marine biologist and researcher, Ernest Just; and physicist and educator, Walter E. Massey.

Their pioneering efforts disproved the racist beliefs that African Americans were not capable of earning advanced degrees in scientific studies, conducting high-level scientific research, or writing papers and articles for professional scientific journals.

After the passage of the 1964 U.S. Civil Rights Bill, educational opportunities and science careers for African Americans significantly increased. More African Americans found meaningful and fulfilling positions at colleges, universities, and research laboratories. An expansion of scholarships and fellowships for African Americans made it possible for greater numbers to earn undergraduate and advanced college degrees.

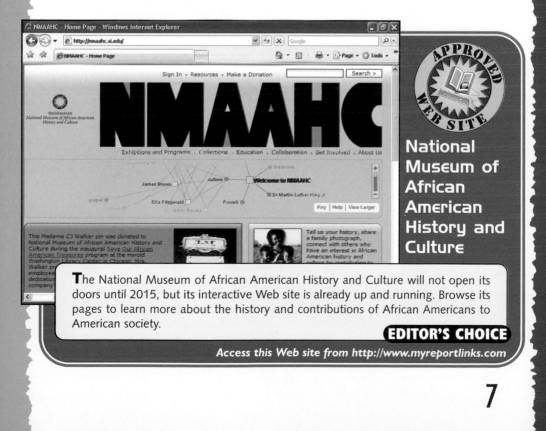

National Museum of African American History and Culture

The National Museum of African American History and Culture will not open its doors until 2015, but its interactive Web site is already up and running. Browse its pages to learn more about the history and contributions of African Americans to American society.

EDITOR'S CHOICE

Access this Web site from http://www.myreportlinks.com

Thanks to the pioneering efforts of African-American scientists and doctors such as Ernest Just and Jane Cooke Wright, careers in any scientific discipline are open to African Americans today.

The advent of space travel and the rapid growth of computer technology have created more opportunities for African Americans in the sciences. John P. Moon made significant contributions in the development of computer disks for saving and retrieving data. Astrophysicist George R. Carruthers has been one of the main forces in the use of ultraviolet light in imaging devices for photographing the moon, stars, and views of Earth from outer space.

In spite of their great progress, the number of African-American scientists is far less than what it could and should be. In 2004, African Americans made up around 12 percent of America's total population. But less than 3 percent of American scientists were African Americans.[1]

The nine African-American scientists profiled here all overcame racial and sometimes economic barriers to make important discoveries and contributions to their fields. They all shared a desire to excel and to help others. And all serve as examples of how dedication can overcome adversity.

Benjamin Banneker

*A*lthough he was a noted inventor, Benjamin Banneker's deeds and concerns extended beyond science and invention. He was also a mathematician, a surveyor, an astronomer, a writer, and a crusader who worked to end racism and slavery.

Lifeline

1759: Inherits the family farm in July.

1731: Born in Baltimore County, Maryland, on November 9.

Chapter 1

Benjamin Banneker was born on November 9, 1731, at his parent's farm near Baltimore, Maryland. His grandmother, Molly Walsh, was white. Molly was born in England and came to America as punishment for a crime she did not commit. She had been working for a farmer milking a cow when the cow kicked over the milk bucket. The farmer accused her of stealing milk and had her arrested.

During her trial, the judge asked Molly if she could read. She proudly said yes. In England at that time, a thief could be sentenced to death. But if an accused criminal was able to read, he or she could be sent to America to serve a sentence. Molly was sent to America to work as an indentured servant on a large tobacco plantation.

1791: Publishes his first almanac.

1806: Dies in Ellicott City, Maryland, on October 25.

1789: Correctly predicts a solar eclipse would occur on April 14.

1797: Publishes his last almanac.

The plantation owner paid for Molly's passage to America, but she had to spend seven years working on his plantation to pay him back. After working off her debt, Molly rented some land and began growing her own tobacco. After a few years, she saved enough money to buy the land and two slaves. One of the slaves was named Bannaka and he claimed to be an African prince. He told Molly he had been captured and sold to slave traders by some of his father's enemies.

After Molly set her slaves free, she married Bannaka. They had a daughter, Mary, who fell in love with a slave named Robert. Molly bought Robert's freedom so he could marry her daughter. The young couple had a son, Benjamin, and adopted Bannak (later changed to Banneker) as their family name.

🧪 BOOKWORM

By using a Bible, Molly taught Benjamin to read and write. When Benjamin was around nine years old, he began attending a school for boys. The school had been established by a religious sect known as the Society of Friends, or Quakers. Benjamin and the rest of the boys in the school only attended classes for a few weeks in the winter. The rest of the year, they had to help their families plant and harvest crops and tend to other duties on the family farm.

The few weeks of formal education that Benjamin received made him curious about the world beyond the family farm. He studied arithmetic and developed an interest in solving math problems and puzzles. Benjamin was more bookish and scholarly than his classmates. He was never very interested in playing or taking part in any childhood games. Benjamin's classmate, Jacob Hall, would later recall how much Benjamin

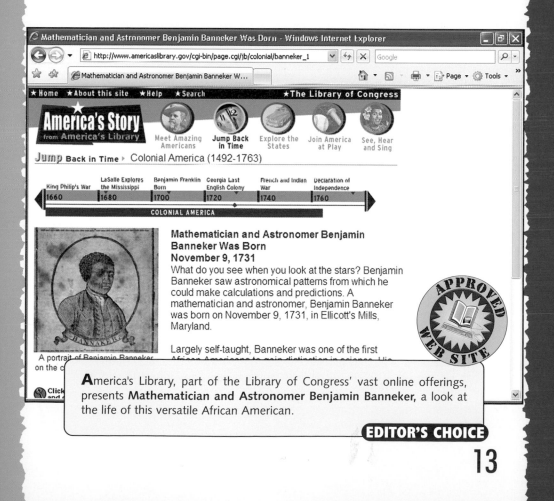

Mathematician and Astronomer Benjamin Banneker Was Born - Windows Internet Explorer

http://www.americaslibrary.gov/cgi-bin/page.cgi/jb/colonial/banneker_1

Google

Mathematician and Astronomer Benjamin Banneker W...

Page ▾ Tools ▾

★Home ★About this site ★Help ★Search ★The Library of Congress

America's Story from America's Library

Meet Amazing Americans | Jump Back in Time | Explore the States | Join America at Play | See, Hear and Sing

Jump Back in Time ▸ Colonial America (1492-1763)

King Philip's War | LaSalle Explores the Mississippi | Benjamin Franklin Born | Georgia Last English Colony | French and Indian War | Declaration of Independence

1660 | 1680 | 1700 | 1720 | 1740 | 1760

COLONIAL AMERICA

Mathematician and Astronomer Benjamin Banneker Was Born
November 9, 1731
What do you see when you look at the stars? Benjamin Banneker saw astronomical patterns from which he could make calculations and predictions. A mathematician and astronomer, Benjamin Banneker was born on November 9, 1731, in Ellicott's Mills, Maryland.

Largely self-taught, Banneker was one of the first African Americans to gain distinction in science. His

A portrait of Benjamin Banneker on the c

APPROVED WEB SITE

America's Library, part of the Library of Congress' vast online offerings, presents **Mathematician and Astronomer Benjamin Banneker,** a look at the life of this versatile African American.

EDITOR'S CHOICE

13

loved reading. "All his delight was to dive into his books," Hall said.[1]

Benjamin's teacher was very impressed by his student's love of reading and desire to learn. He loaned Benjamin college-level books from his own library. Benjamin read histories of ancient Greece and Rome and books written by mathematicians.

Unfortunately, Benjamin's formal education ended after only one or two years. The demands of helping out on the family farm made any further schooling impossible.

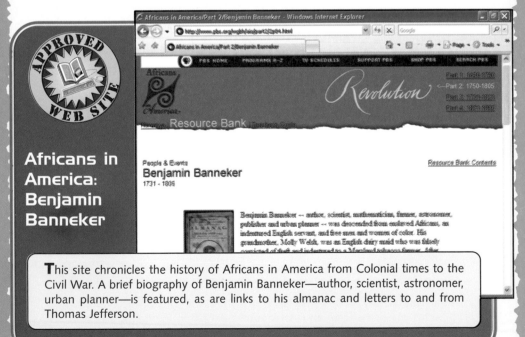

Africans in America: Benjamin Banneker

This site chronicles the history of Africans in America from Colonial times to the Civil War. A brief biography of Benjamin Banneker—author, scientist, astronomer, urban planner—is featured, as are links to his almanac and letters to and from Thomas Jefferson.

Access this Web site from http://www.myreportlinks.com

🧪 BANNEKER'S FIRST CLOCK

When he was not working on the family farm, Benjamin Banneker spent much of his free time studying the movements of the sun and the stars. Looking at the sky was how Banneker could determine the time of day. The workday began when the sun rose and ended when it set. When the sun reached its highest point in the sky, it was time for the noon meal.

Banneker was fascinated with the concept of time and he wanted to have a machine that precisely measured it. In Colonial America in the 1750s, only the wealthiest people owned watches or clocks. Banneker decided that if someone would loan him a timepiece, he could learn how it worked. Then, he could build a clock of his own.

Some unknown benefactor loaned Banneker his watch. At first, Banneker was afraid to take the watch apart. He thought he might accidentally destroy the mechanism. Finally, he pried off the back of the watch and looked at the tiny gears, springs, and balances that made it run.

Banneker then began making detailed drawings of the watch's parts and computing the exact scale for making the parts to construct a clock. He carefully hand carved each piece from wood that he had treated and saved. He used brass to build the machine parts. After months of painstaking labor, Benjamin Banneker had his clock.

The clock ran perfectly. Every hour, a small iron bell he had added to it chimed. Word of Banneker's chiming clock spread through the Maryland countryside. Scores of people came to the Banneker's farm to see it.

In July 1759, Benjamin Banneker's father died. At the age of twenty-eight, Benjamin Banneker became the sole owner of the family farm. For about the next twelve years, his life was dominated by work on the farm. He had little time to pursue his scientific and intellectual interests. His scant leisure time was used for playing musical instruments, reading his Bible, and solving math puzzles.

CHARTS AND PREDICTIONS

Sometime in January 1771, a pair of brothers, John and Andrew Ellicott, began constructing a gristmill on some land close to Banneker's farm. After they got their mill going, the Ellicott brothers opened a general store, which became sort of a community center. Banneker often visited the store, and he became a good friend of the Ellicott family, especially eighteen-year-old George.

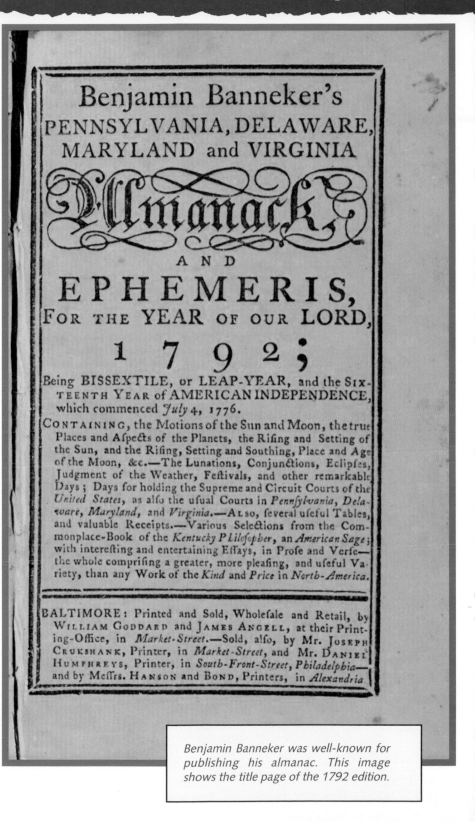

Benjamin Banneker was well-known for publishing his almanac. This image shows the title page of the 1792 edition.

Banneker and George Ellicott shared a strong mutual interest in literature, science, math, and astronomy. Ellicott loaned Banneker books on astronomy and math, and when he had to leave on a long business trip, Ellicott let Banneker borrow his telescope and some surveying tools.

For Benjamin Banneker, tending the family farm took a backseat to learning about astronomy. He used the borrowed telescope to study the constellations and the phases of the moon.

This *TIME Magazine*: **Benjamin Banneker** article examines African-American scientist Benjamin Banneker's letter in 1791 to then-Secretary of State Thomas Jefferson, criticizing Jefferson's ownership of slaves.

He built a cabin with a skylight so he could study the stars and make astronomical calculations.

Banneker got a reputation for accurately charting and predicting the movements of the Sun, the stars, Moon, and Earth. He predicted that a solar eclipse would occur on April 14, 1789. Other noted astronomers had calculated a different date, but Banneker believed that their work was flawed. He was correct. On April 14, as Banneker predicted, a solar eclipse occurred.

ALMANACS AND MORE

In 1791, Banneker wrote and published the first of several almanacs. It was called *Benjamin Banneker's Pennsylvania, Delaware, Maryland and Virginia Almanack and Ephemerris.* It contained information on the weather, lunar phases, times for the sunrise and sunset, tides, eclipses, and medicines.

Banneker's almanac also contained articles denouncing slavery. As a free African American, Banneker felt a need to speak against the practice of holding other African Americans in bondage. He sent a copy to Thomas Jefferson, who was then serving as George Washington's secretary of state. Banneker knew that Jefferson owned slaves and he asked Jefferson how he could justify slavery.

19

▲ Benjamin Banneker is also known for having surveyed Washington, D.C. This image shows the Washington Monument—part of the National Mall.

Jefferson never did free his slaves or denounce slavery, but he began corresponding with Banneker. In his letters, Jefferson acknowledged Banneker's intellectual achievements, and he acknowledged that African Americans deserved better treatment.

Along with his almanacs, Banneker is remembered for surveying the city of Washington, D.C. Legend has it that he helped design the nation's capital, but modern historians say that is not true.

Banneker continued to publish his almanacs until 1797. Declining sales and the infirmities of aging forced him to cease publication. Still, he continued to make astronomical observations and records until his death on October 25, 1806.

George R. Carruthers

George R. Carruthers is someone who has always been fascinated with watching the stars. That fascination has made him a renowned astrophysicist and professor. His motto, "Not even the sky is the limit to what a person can accomplish,"[1] has inspired his students to follow his example of achievement and accomplishment.

George Carruthers was born in Cincinnati, Ohio, on October 1, 1939. His father, also

Lifeline

1961: Receives BS in physics from the University of Illinois.

1964: Receives doctorate in astronautical engineering from the University of Illinois.

1939: Born in Cincinnati, Ohio, on October 1.

1962: Receives masters in nuclear engineering from the University of Illinois.

Chapter 2

named George, was a civil engineer who encouraged his oldest child to pursue his interest in science. As a boy, George was an avid reader of science-fiction books and comics. One of his early inspirations was the comic-book hero Buck Rogers, a fictional space traveler who was the first comic-book character to go to Mars.

When he was ten, George began working on projects that would indicate the direction his life would take. Using the money he made from working as a delivery boy, George made his own telescope. He ordered the lenses from a mail-order company and mounted them in a cardboard tube he found at his house.

1973: Awarded the Warner Prize from the American Astronomical Society.

1972: Earns NASA's Exceptional Achievement Scientific Award.

1987: Named Black Engineer of the Year.

The telescope worked even better than George expected. He spent more of his free time gazing at the stars and reading his father's books on astronomy. He also began building model rockets.

George's life took an unexpected turn when his father died. George was only twelve. Since they had relatives living in Chicago, George's family moved there. His mother, Sophia, supported her four children by working for the U.S. Postal Service.

At Englewood High School in Chicago, the science teachers took notice of George's intelligence and his passion for science. They saw that

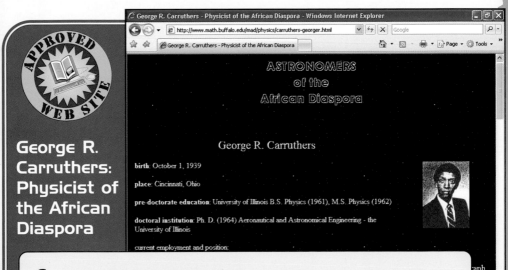

George R. Carruthers: Physicist of the African Diaspora

George R. Carruthers - Physicist of the African Diaspora - Windows Internet Explorer

http://www.math.buffalo.edu/mad/physics/carruthers-georger.html

Google

George R. Carruthers - Physicist of the African Diaspora

Page ▾ Tools ▾

ASTRONOMERS of the African Diaspora

George R. Carruthers

birth: October 1, 1939

place: Cincinnati, Ohio

pre-doctorate education: University of Illinois B.S. Physics (1961), M.S. Physics (1962)

doctoral institution: Ph. D. (1964) Aeronautical and Astronomical Engineering - the University of Illinois

current employment and position:

George Carruthers, an astrophysicist whose cameras and imaging devices have been used by NASA, is profiled in this university site hosted by a mathematics professor.

Access this Web site from http://www.myreportlinks.com

George had a lot of potential. His teachers encouraged him by showing him local science resources like the Museum of Science and Industry and the Chicago Planetarium.

George's teachers also encouraged him with his telescope projects. Their encouragement spurred George to build a telescope that won first prize in the local science-fair competition.

In 1957, George enrolled at the College of Engineering at the University of Illinois. He was an excellent student and he earned three degrees in just seven years. George received a BS in physics in 1961, a MS in nuclear engineering in 1962, and a PhD in aeronautical and astronautical engineering in 1964.

While George was attending college, astronomy was becoming an important part of America's space program. Scientists were thinking that astronomical studies could be done in space. Satellites, both manned and unmanned, launched into space could serve as astronomical stations. In space, telescopes would have a clearer view of the stars and planets because they would be outside of Earth's atmosphere.

After receiving his doctoral degree, George Carruthers was hired by the U.S. Navy to work at the U.S. Naval Research Laboratory. The Naval Research Laboratory is a well-known

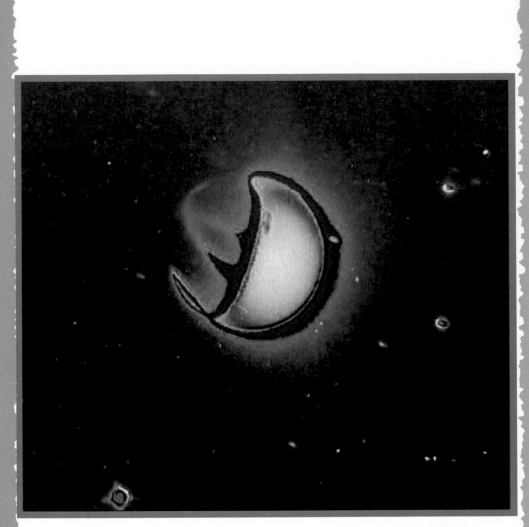

▲ *An ultraviolet image of Earth taken from the Moon with Carruthers's telescope.*

facility where scientists can engage in advanced research. Carruthers became involved in research that combined his interests in astronomy and space travel.

⚗ BREAKING THE LIMITS

George Carruthers's first project was the development of a space camera that could measure ultraviolet light. Ultraviolet light is useful to astronomers because it is used to find out which molecules and atoms are present in the thin gas between the stars. Ultraviolet light has also been used to identify the molecules and atoms found in the gases that make up a comet's tail.

Even though Carruthers had a team of engineers, technicians, and scientists helping him, it took several years to design and build the camera. After the camera passed all of its tests, it traveled to the Moon during the 1972 *Apollo 16* mission. *Apollo 16* commander John W. Young put the camera on the Moon's surface. The camera took pictures of interstellar gases and of Earth's atmosphere.

The pictures of the earth's atmosphere were used to determine the concentration of pollutants like carbon monoxide above large cities. It was a pioneering achievement in space astronomy.

The *Apollo 16* spaceflight was the first mission on which cameras designed by George Carruthers and his team were used. This is an image of *Apollo 16* taking off from the Kennedy Space Center on April 16, 1972.

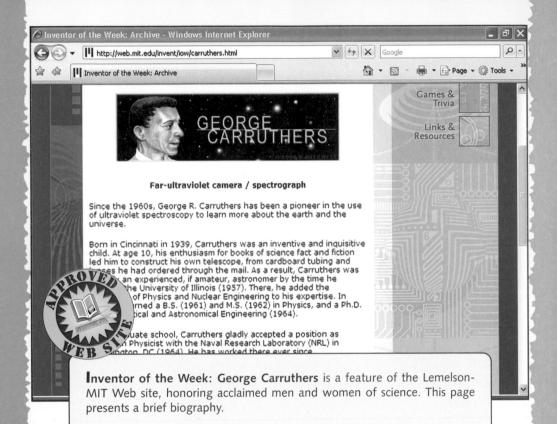

Inventor of the Week: George Carruthers is a feature of the Lemelson-MIT Web site, honoring acclaimed men and women of science. This page presents a brief biography.

"People sort of expected to see what we saw, but even so, just having the first pictures that actually verified that was very exciting," Carruthers said. ". . . One of the things that makes it very exciting and interesting is that in the early days of the space program almost every flight was something that was breaking new ground—especially in the astronomy area where we were previously limited to telescopes from the ground."[2]

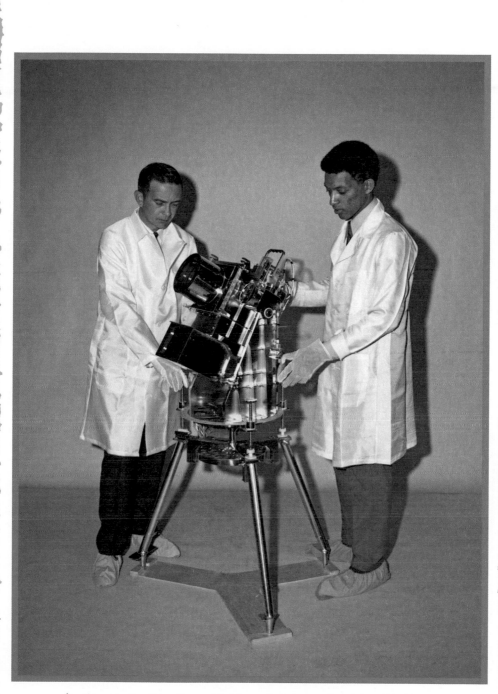

▲ *George R. Carruthers (right) and Commander John W. Young demonstrate Carruthers's imaging telescope.*

🧪 CAMERAMAN

Since *Apollo 16,* cameras built and designed by Carruthers's teams have been used by the space shuttle to make exact measurements of the ozone layer surrounding Earth. Exact measurements are important because the ozone layer filters out portions of the sun's ultraviolet radiation that are harmful to human, plant, and animal life. Scientists believe that the ozone layer is reduced by polluting gases, so precise measurements are useful in setting environmental regulations.

This camera was also responsible for helping detect the presence of hydrogen in deep space.

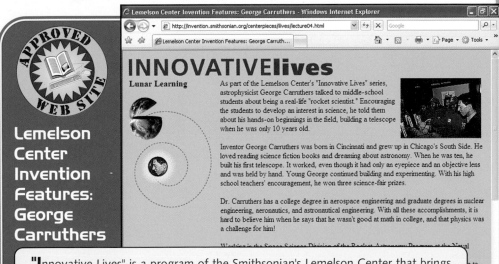

Lemelson Center Invention Features: George Carruthers

INNOVATIVElives

Lunar Learning

As part of the Lemelson Center's "Innovative Lives" series, astrophysicist George Carruthers talked to middle-school students about being a real-life "rocket scientist." Encouraging the students to develop an interest in science, he told them about his hands-on beginnings in the field, building a telescope when he was only 10 years old.

Inventor George Carruthers was born in Cincinnati and grew up in Chicago's South Side. He loved reading science fiction books and dreaming about astronomy. When he was ten, he built his first telescope. It worked, even though it had only an eyepiece and an objective lens and was held by hand. Young George continued building and experimenting. With his high school teachers' encouragement, he won three science-fair prizes.

Dr. Carruthers has a college degree in aerospace engineering and graduate degrees in nuclear engineering, aeronautics, and astronautical engineering. With all these accomplishments, it is hard to believe him when he says that he wasn't good at math in college, and that physics was a challenge for him!

"Innovative Lives" is a program of the Smithsonian's Lemelson Center that brings scientists into the classroom. This page offers an introduction to George Carruthers, an acclaimed astrophysicist whose cameras have been used in space missions.

Access this Web site from http://www.myreportlinks.com

That important discovery showed that plants were not the only source of the earth's oxygen. The discovery also led to new theories of how the stars originated.

George Carruthers has also been a pioneer in the use and development of electronic telescopes used by the National Aeronautics and Space Administration (NASA). These telescopes are used to transform light from planets and distant stars into electrical signals that are transmitted back to Earth. Those signals create images that can be displayed on television monitors.

Most recently, Carruthers and his team have developed computer-controlled cameras for space missions. The images and information that come through the lenses are read by a computer. Images and data gathered by these cameras can be used to help determine how new planets and stars can be formed from the gases and dusts that compose most of the known universe.

DEEDS AND ACCOMPLISHMENTS

While Carruthers's main focus has been on conducting research and designing cameras, he still teaches classes in astrophysics when his schedule allows it. He also works with other minority engineers and scientists through the National Technical Association (NTA). The NTA provides

This radio telescope sits atop the Naval Research Laboratory administration building. It is here that George Carruthers began the work that led to the development of his ultraviolet camera.

minority youth with information on careers in scientific and technical fields. The organization also encourages minority youth to pursue careers in those fields.

During his career, Carruthers has received numerous awards. Among them are the Black Engineer of the Year Award in 1987, the Exceptional Achievement Scientific Award from NASA in 1972, and the Warner Prize from the American Astronomical Society in 1973.

Married since 1973, Carruthers is known as a private person who prefers to give credit to his coworkers instead of claiming it for himself. He continues to work at the Naval Research Laboratory and to promote interest in science and technical careers for young African Americans.

Charles R. Drew

To simply call Charles Richard Drew a scientist ignores his many other achievements. He is remembered as a dedicated and accomplished teacher, surgeon, researcher, and humanitarian. His landmark work in the use and storage of blood plasma for emergency needs saved thousands of lives in World War II. It earned him the title Father of Blood Plasma.

Drew was born in Washington, D.C., on June 3, 1904. He was the oldest son of Richard T. and Nora Drew's five

Lifeline

1912: His sister dies in a flu epidemic, inspiring him to devote his life to science.

1933: Receives Doctor of Medicine and Master of Surgery degrees from McGill University Medical School.

1904: Born in Washington, D.C., on June 3.

1926: Receives degree from Amherst College.

children. Richard worked as a carpet layer and Nora taught school before Charles was born. Charles grew up in a cultured, close-knit, religious family.

♦ AN ALL-AROUND STAR

Chapter

3

In high school, Charles was both an excellent student and a gifted athlete. At Paul Laurence Dunbar High School he won letters in four different sports. During his senior year at Dunbar, Charles was honored as the school's best athlete, the most popular student, and as the student who did the most for the school.

Charles's athletic talents earned him a scholarship at Amherst College in Massachusetts. He continued to excel in sports. Charles was captain of the track team and was honored for being the most valuable player on

1950: Killed in car accident near Burlington, North Carolina, on April 1.

1980: U.S. Postal Service issues a stamp in his honor.

1944: Wins the Spingarn Medal from the NAACP.

1976: First African American to have portrait displayed at the Clinical Center of the National Institutes of Health.

37

the football team. Still, sports were secondary to studying and making good grades. Charles was determined to go on to medical school and then become a doctor.

A career in medicine was not Charles Drew's original plan when he first started college. He initially set out to be an engineer. However, certain events influenced his decision to make the switch. One began with a leg injury while playing football in high school. The injury led to a serious infection that put him in the hospital and on the operating table. As a result of that injury,

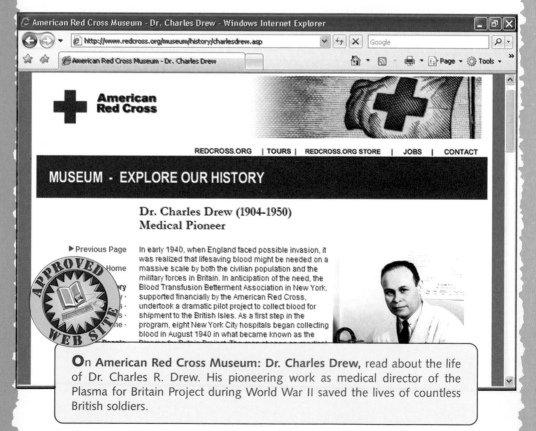

American Red Cross Museum - Dr. Charles Drew - Windows Internet Explorer

http://www.redcross.org/museum/history/charlesdrew.asp   Google

American Red Cross Museum - Dr. Charles Drew   Page ▾   Tools ▾

American Red Cross

REDCROSS.ORG | TOURS | REDCROSS.ORG STORE | JOBS | CONTACT

MUSEUM · EXPLORE OUR HISTORY

Dr. Charles Drew (1904-1950)
Medical Pioneer

▶ Previous Page

Home

In early 1940, when England faced possible invasion, it was realized that lifesaving blood might be needed on a massive scale by both the civilian population and the military forces in Britain. In anticipation of the need, the Blood Transfusion Betterment Association in New York, supported financially by the American Red Cross, undertook a dramatic pilot project to collect blood for shipment to the British Isles. As a first step in the program, eight New York City hospitals began collecting blood in August 1940 in what became known as the

On **American Red Cross Museum: Dr. Charles Drew,** read about the life of Dr. Charles R. Drew. His pioneering work as medical director of the Plasma for Britain Project during World War II saved the lives of countless British soldiers.

Drew told a magazine he "wanted to know how the body works." Also in 1920, his sister fell victim to a great influenza epidemic. "No one seemed to be able to stop it and people died by the hundreds every week. I have studied the sciences diligently since that time."[1]

ROADBLOCKS

When he graduated from Amherst in 1926, Charles Drew had the grades to get into medical school, but he did not have the money. He took a job teaching and coaching at Morgan State College in Baltimore, Maryland. Drew taught biology and chemistry, as well as coaching and serving as Morgan's director of athletics.

In 1928, Drew applied to medical school at Harvard University and Howard University. At that time, those two universities were about the only medical schools in the United States that accepted African Americans. Howard rejected Drew because he did not have enough credits in English. Harvard accepted him, but they told him he could not enroll immediately. He had to wait a year.

Charles Drew did not want to wait. He applied and was accepted at McGill University in Montreal, Canada. At McGill, Drew continued to be both a standout athlete and student. He was captain of the track team and he also won several academic honors.

In spite of his athletic and academic successes, Drew did not have an easy time in medical school. A lack of money was a constant concern. He worked as a waiter and busboy in the school cafeteria. The little money he made from that part-time job did not go far. On New Year's Day 1930, Drew wrote:

> Today I haven't been hungry . . . I am not sick and have no great sorrow, yet I have felt poverty

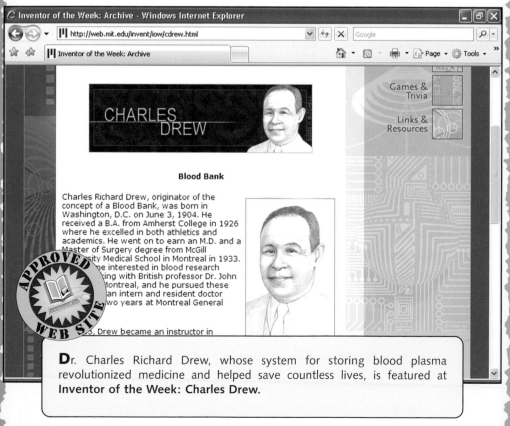

Dr. Charles Richard Drew, whose system for storing blood plasma revolutionized medicine and helped save countless lives, is featured at **Inventor of the Week: Charles Drew.**

today as I have never felt if before. I have a dollar. Tonight I wanted to join the merry-making in some form or another so bad that my heart ached. I couldn't go very far on a dollar, . . . [and] I am afraid to spend it—tomorrow I must eat and the day after, and many days after that. . . . For days now I have not been sure whether I would eat or not.[2]

🧪 BANKING BLOOD

Charles Drew graduated second in a class of 137 and received MD (Medical Doctor) and CM (Master of Surgery) degrees from McGill. Then he served a one-year internship and a one-year residency at Montreal General Hospital. During that time, he practiced medicine under the supervision of an experienced doctor. In 1935, he passed the test of the National Board of Medical Examiners and joined the faculty of the Howard University School of Medicine.

At Howard, Drew taught students about the symptoms, causes, and treatments of different diseases. He enjoyed teaching and inspiring other African Americans to become doctors, but he wanted to become a surgeon. A fellowship enabled him to study surgery at the Columbia University Medical School.

While attending Columbia, Drew began working with other doctors on solving the problem of long-term blood storage for transfusions. As early as 1918, an English doctor had suggested that plasma could be used instead of whole blood for emergency transfusions. Drew's research convinced him that plasma could be substituted for whole blood.

Whole blood is made up of four elements— white and red blood cells, platelets, and plasma. Plasma is a clear yellowish liquid comprised of important minerals and proteins that transport both types of blood cells and the platelets throughout the body. When whole blood is given, the blood type of the donated blood and of the person receiving the blood have to match. This is determined largely by red blood cells. Since plasma alone does not contain red blood cells, it can be given to anyone with any blood type.

Drew discovered that plasma was easier to store and preserve than whole blood. Whole blood could only be stored for a few days before the red cells began breaking down. Plasma could be stored and preserved for months before going bad.

In 1940, Drew published his thesis for his degree. It was entitled "Banked Blood: A Study of Blood Preservation." In his thesis, Drew said that blood banks should be storing

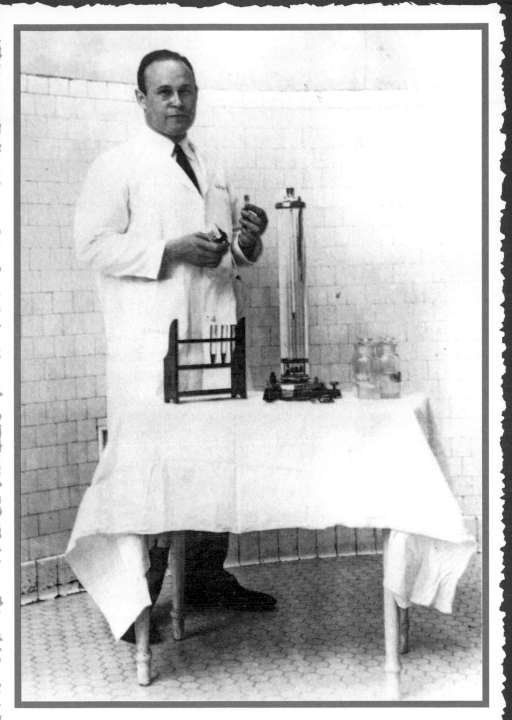

▲ *Drew's discoveries made it possible to store blood for months, rather than days, before it went bad. This development saved thousands of lives during World War II.*

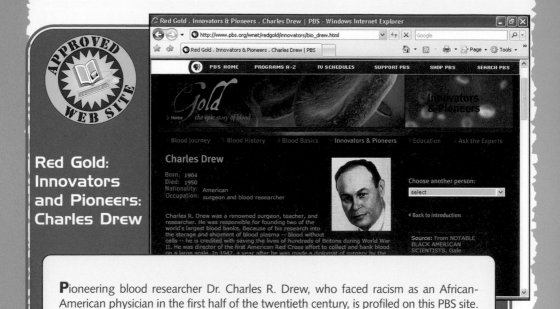

APPROVED WEB SITE

Red Gold:
Innovators
and Pioneers:
Charles Drew

Charles Drew

Born: 1904
Died: 1950
Nationality: American
Occupation: surgeon and blood researcher

Charles R. Drew was a renowned surgeon, teacher, and researcher. He was responsible for founding two of the world's largest blood banks. Because of his research into the storage and shipment of blood plasma -- blood without cells -- he is credited with saving the lives of hundreds of Britons during World War II. He was director of the first American Red Cross effort to collect and bank blood on a large scale. In 1942, a year after he was made a diplomat of surgery by the

Choose another person:
select

◂ Back to introduction

Source: From NOTABLE
BLACK AMERICAN
SCIENTISTS, Gale

Pioneering blood researcher Dr. Charles R. Drew, who faced racism as an African-American physician in the first half of the twentieth century, is profiled on this PBS site.

Access this Web site from http://www.myreportlinks.com

plasma instead of whole blood. With his research team helping him, Drew demonstrated that plasma could be stored for months at a time. Unlike whole blood, plasma did not need to be refrigerated to keep from spoiling.

Drew's discoveries and research were very timely and helped save thousands of lives. World War II had begun in 1939. Although the United States would not enter the war until 1941, there was a dire need for blood plasma in Britain. The Germans were constantly bombing Britain, which caused thousands of civilian and military casualties. Drew was put in charge of a program called Blood for Britain.

Before Drew took over the program, much of the plasma being shipped to Britain was spoiled when it got there. The British hospitals and blood banks were not experienced in collecting and preserving plasma. They did not know how to keep the plasma free of disease-causing organisms.

Drew set up uniform standards for collecting blood and storing plasma. He also established a laboratory that examined and ensured the quality of the plasma being sent to Britain. Thanks to Drew's work, there was a dramatic decrease in spoiled plasma reaching Britain.

The British began using Drew's high quality standards. Soon, they were able to set up their own national blood bank program for stockpiling valuable plasma. By that time, Drew was serving as the director of the American Red Cross Blood Bank. He was asked to organize a blood drive of a million donors to aid the American war effort.

Unfortunately, racial issues caused Drew to resign from that important position. At that time, the armed forces had a policy that excluded African Americans from being blood donors. In his resignation statement, Drew spoke out against that policy.

▲ This laboratory technician is looking through samples in a blood bank in hopes of finding a match for a patient.

"I feel that the ruling of the United States Army and Navy regarding the refusal of colored blood donors is an indefensible one from any point of view. There is no scientific basis for the separation of the blood of different races except on the basis of the individual blood types or groups."[3]

After his resignation, Drew returned to Howard University Medical School as a professor of surgery. He also worked as the chief surgeon and medical director at the Freedmen's Hospital in Washington, D.C. In 1944 the National Association for the Advancement of Colored People (NAACP) awarded him their Spingarn Medal for his outstanding work in the teaching and training of African-American doctors.

A SHORT LIFE, A LONG LEGACY

Charles Drew's life tragically ended when he was only forty-five years old. On April 1, 1950, he apparently fell asleep at the wheel while driving to a medical meeting in Tuskegee, Alabama. Three other doctors were traveling with him, but none of them were seriously injured.

It was later reported that Drew died because the doctors at a white North Carolina hospital were inattentive. The story claimed that Drew bled to death. According to Dr. John R. Ford, a

47

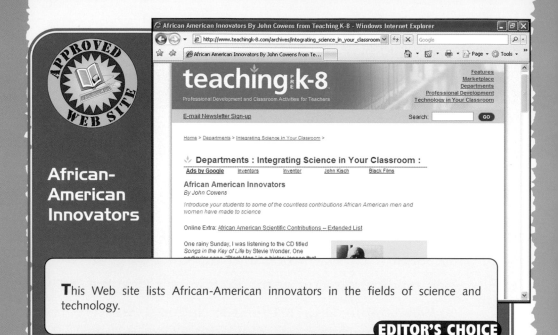

APPROVED WEB SITE

African-American Innovators

African American Innovators By John Cowens from Teaching K-8 - Windows Internet Explorer

http://www.teachingk-8.com/archives/integrating_science_in_your_classroom

Google

African American Innovators By John Cowens from Te...

Page ▾   Tools ▾

teaching k-8

Professional Development and Classroom Activities for Teachers

Features
Marketplace
Departments
Professional Development
Technology in Your Classroom

E-mail Newsletter Sign-up

Search: GO

Home > Departments > Integrating Science in Your Classroom >

Departments : Integrating Science in Your Classroom :

Ads by Google   Inventors   Inventor   John Kisch   Black Films

African American Innovators
By John Cowens

Introduce your students to some of the countless contributions African American men and women have made to science

Online Extra: African American Scientific Contributions – Extended List

One rainy Sunday, I was listening to the CD titled *Songs in the Key of Life* by Stevie Wonder. One particular song, "Black Man," is a history lesson that

This Web site lists African-American innovators in the fields of science and technology.

EDITOR'S CHOICE

Access this Web site from http://www.myreportlinks.com

passenger in Drew's car, that story simply was not true.

Drew had a broken neck and his chest was crushed. The accident had also ruptured the veins known as the venae cavae that return deoxygenated blood from the body into the heart. They both empty into the right atrium of the heart. Those severe injuries made a blood transfusion impossible.

"All the blood in the world could not have saved him," Ford said.[4]

In spite of his short life, Drew has left a legacy of achievement in lifesaving techniques and in the training of African-American doctors.

In 1976, Drew's portrait was displayed at the Clinical Center of the National Institutes of Health. He became the first African American to join its portrait gallery of famous scientists. In 1980 the U.S. Postal Service honored Charles Drew by issuing a stamp honoring him as part of its "Great Americans" series.

Shirley Ann Jackson

African-American physicist Shirley Ann Jackson studies a world within a world, within a world. Jackson's specialty is subatomic particles. A molecule is one of the smallest units of matter. Molecules are composed of two or more atoms. Within an atom are subatomic particles even smaller than the atom.

Lifeline

1968: Receives BS in physics from the Massachusetts Institute of Technology.

1974: Becomes visiting scientist at the European Center for Nuclear Research.

1946: Born in Washington, D.C., on August 5.

1973: Receives doctorate in physics from the Massachusetts Institute of Technology.

Shirley was born in Washington, D.C., on August 5, 1946. Her parents, George and Beatrice, recognized and encouraged Shirley's interest in science. Both parents put a high value on seeing that Shirley obtained a good education. George helped her with science projects and encouraged Shirley to aim high and think big. He often would tell her to "aim for the stars so that you can reach the treetops, and at least you'll get off the ground."[1]

Beatrice inspired Shirley by reading her stories about famous African Americans. Shirley learned about the lives and accomplishments of astronomer/mathematician Benjamin Banneker, educator Mary McLeod Bethune, and poet Paul Laurence Dunbar.

Along with her parents' strong support, Shirley was motivated by her curiosity in the pursuit of scientific knowledge. "My goal was

Chapter 4

1995: President Clinton appoints her to head Nuclear Regulatory Commission.

1985: Begins serving on New Jersey Commission on Science and Technology.

1999: Becomes president of Rensselaer Polytechnic Institute.

Shirley Ann Jackson graduated from the Massachusetts Institute of Technology (MIT) in 1968. This image is of the Ray and Maria Stata Center, a famous building on the MIT campus.

always to pursue the physics opportunities and however great or non-great I might turn out to be, I thought it was important to be in an exciting place, to work on exciting problems," Jackson said. "What science gives you is the chance to be the one who uncovers the unknown, who creates the new paradigm. And all along the way there are all the little thrills having to do with the little discoveries you make—and there's a lot of satisfaction."[2]

Shirley's interest in science continued to blossom at Theodore Roosevelt High School. She took advanced placement classes in both science and

In 2005, *Time Magazine* called Dr. Jackson "the ultimate role model for women in science." Titled **NSF.gov News: Shirley Ann Jackson**, this National Science Foundation News Web page chronicles her impressive career.

math. Shirley also competed in science fairs and won awards for projects. She was first in her class when she graduated from Roosevelt in 1964.

🜂 KEEPING FOCUS

Shirley's excellent grades and glowing references from her teachers helped her to get accepted to the Massachusetts Institute of Technology (MIT) in Cambridge, Massachusetts. MIT is a very competitive school with very high admission standards.

When Jackson entered MIT in 1964, there were only about a dozen African-American students among the school's enrollment of four thousand. At first, Jackson found it hard to make friends at MIT. Some students refused to sit near her. One faculty member tried to make her feel that she did not belong at MIT by suggesting that she "learn a trade."[3] Jackson spent a lot of time studying alone in her room.

Her social life improved after she joined a sorority. Her sorority sisters gave Jackson a circle of friends to support and encourage her. As a member of her sorority, Jackson tutored high-school students. That started her long involvement in teaching and helping young people.

Even with a full load of classes and sorority activities, Jackson took on other tasks. She did

In 1999, Dr. Jackson became president of Rensselaer Polytechnic Institute, a private research university located in Troy, New York.

volunteer work at Boston City Hospital. She also worked with the Black Student Union (BSU) and the MIT administration to help recruit more minority students.

Shirley Jackson received her BS in physics from MIT in 1968. Her academic achievements were noticed by other universities. Harvard, Brown, and the University of Chicago all tried to get her to enroll for graduate work. She decided to stay at MIT to continue studying physics and recruit minority students.

As a graduate student, Shirley Jackson enjoyed some improved financial security. She received a three-year traineeship from the National Science Foundation. Jackson was also the recipient of several fellowships from the Ford Foundation.

When she received her PhD in physics in 1973, she became the first African-American woman to earn a doctoral degree from MIT. She also became just the second African-American woman to receive a doctorate in physics. Jackson was quickly hired as a research associate at the Fermi National Accelerator Laboratory. She did research in particle physics and subatomic particles. She studied how the basic particles of matter interact with one another.

🧪 CHANGING FOCUS

In 1974, Shirley Jackson left her research associate job to become a visiting scientist at the
European Center for Nuclear Research (CERN)
in Switzerland. Two years later, she joined the
technical staff at Bell Telephone Laboratories. At
Bell Labs, she shifted her research from particle
to solid state physics. In solid state physics, scientists study what happens when atoms are
joined together to make a solid. After sixteen
years with Bell Labs, Jackson went to Rutgers
University in New Jersey to serve as a professor
of physics. She continued to work at Bell Labs as
a consultant. While at Rutgers, Jackson taught
undergraduate and graduate students and
advised doctoral students. She continued her
research with the assistance of the students she
was mentoring.

"As a researcher, you have more ideas than
you can work on yourself," Jackson noted. "Rutgers gave me the opportunity to build a research
group with young people, to educate them, and
to make them partners in research."[4]

Even though she was very busy with teaching
and research, Jackson found time for government service. In 1985, she was appointed to the
New Jersey Commission on Science and Technology by Governor Thomas Kean. She worked

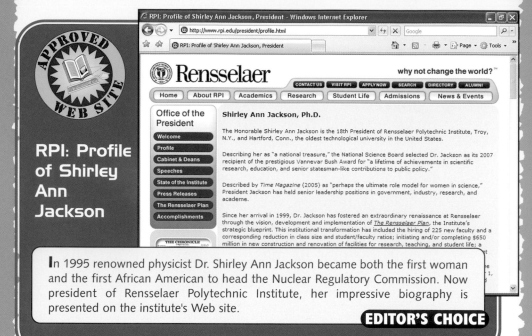

RPI: Profile of Shirley Ann Jackson

In 1995 renowned physicist Dr. Shirley Ann Jackson became both the first woman and the first African American to head the Nuclear Regulatory Commission. Now president of Rensselaer Polytechnic Institute, her impressive biography is presented on the institute's Web site.

EDITOR'S CHOICE

Access this Web site from http://www.myreportlinks.com

to build relationships among state schools and private industrial organizations. Together, they worked on solutions to common problems like the disposal of hazardous waste and improved manufacturing methods for science and technological businesses.

HEADING THE NRC

Shirley Jackson's work on the New Jersey Commission on Science attracted the attention of President Bill Clinton. In 1995, he appointed her to head the Nuclear Regulatory Commission (NRC). When she was appointed, the NRC had

▲ *In 2007, Jackson received the Vannevar Bush Award from the National Science Board for "a lifetime of achievement in scientific research."*

more than three thousand employees and a budget of almost a half a billion dollars.

The major functions of the NRC are to ensure that the use of nuclear energy does not threaten the health and safety of the public. The agency also renews and issues licenses for nuclear power plants, oversees the use of radiation in medicine and scientific research, and develops standards for the safe disposal of nuclear waste.

Shirley Jackson became the first woman and the first African American to head the NRC. In a 1999 article in *Black Issues in Higher Education,* Michele Collison praised Shirley Jackson's work by writing: "Jackson has won considerable praise for restoring credibility to a troubled agency and increasing the agency's oversight over several nuclear power plants."[5]

SCIENTIST, EDUCATOR, AND LEADER

In 1999, Shirley Jackson left the NRC to become the president of Rensselaer Polytechnic Institute (RPI) in Troy, New York. Her appointment was yet another first in her career as a scientist and educator. She became the first African-American woman to head a major research university.

As president of RPI, Jackson has made it a personal goal to recruit more African-American and women students. She has also worked to

Science Update: Spotlight on African American Scientists - Windows Internet Explorer

http://www.scienceupdate.com/spotlights/africanamerican.php   Google

Science Update: Spotlight on African American Scientists

Science Update

HOME   ABOUT   ARCHIVES   PODCAST   CONTACT

SEAR

SPOTLIGHT   African American Scientists

Sponsored by Delta SEE
Science and Everyday Experiences Initiative   SEE Δ_{Σ_Θ}

SPOTLIGHT on   Since Benjamin Banneker and George Washington Carver left their

This site from the American Association for the Advancement of Science looks at some current African-American scientists who have become distinguished in their fields.

EDITOR'S CHOICE

Science Update: Spotlight on African-American Scientists

Access this Web site from http://www.myreportlinks.com

bring additional African Americans to the faculty. She sees that there is clearly a need to bring more women and minorities into careers in math and science.

"As president of a major university, I will have a platform to speak out broadly about the need to prepare more women and minorities for math and science careers," Jackson said.[6]

Ernest Everett Just

Ernest Everett Just dedicated his life to teaching, as well as conducting important groundbreaking research in zoology and marine biology. His research on the development of both fertilization as well as how eggs developed without fertilization—a process known as parthogenesis —was quite significant.

Lifeline

1907: Earns BS in biology from Dartmouth College.

1916: Receives PhD in zoology from the Universit of Chicago.

1883: Born in Charleston, South Carolina, on August 14.

1907: Begins teaching at Howard University.

Chapter 5

But his discovery of the role that protoplasm plays in cell development is considered his most important achievement. Just and his work became so respected by other scientists that they would often refer to him as "a scientist's scientist."[1]

Ernest Just was born on August 14, 1883, in Charleston, South Carolina. His father, Charles, was a dock builder and his mother, Mary, worked as a teacher. Ernest was only four years old when his father died. Mary took charge of Ernest's education by sending him to the Colored Normal Industrial, Agricultural and Mechanical College in Orangeburg, South Carolina. Today, that school is known as South Carolina State University.

1933: Forced to flee from the Nazis.

1941: Dies on October 27, 1941, in Washington, D.C.

1930: Moves to Germany to teach at Kaiser Wilhelm Institute.

1940: Returns to Howard University.

🧪 SCHOOLWORK AND TEACHING

When he was sixteen, Ernest left South Carolina to attend Kimball Union Academy in New Hampshire. Ernest excelled academically. He finished the four-year course in three years, graduating as the top student in the class of 1903. While at Kimball, he was president of the debating society and the editor of the school newspaper.

After leaving Kimball, Ernest Just enrolled at nearby Dartmouth College in Hanover, New

Unsung Heroes: Ernest Everett Just focuses on African Americans whose contributions to society have not received the credit they deserve. The site includes a biography of biologist Ernest Everett Just, an unsung hero of science.

Hampshire. He was the only African American in a freshman class of 288 students. After taking his first science class at Dartmouth, Just decided to major in biology.

By the time he graduated in 1907, Just had taken every science class offered at Dartmouth. He was the only student in that graduating class to receive magna cum laude (with great distinction) honors for his academic achievements.

In the fall of 1907, Just began his teaching career at Howard University. Originally, he was an instructor in English and rhetoric (public speaking), but in 1909 the focus of his academic career changed. Just began taking graduate level courses in biology at the Marine Biological Laboratory (MBL) in Woods Hole, Massachusetts. After several summers of studying there, Just earned a PhD in zoology from the University of Chicago in 1916.

By the time Just completed his doctoral studies, he had published several research papers in biological and scientific journals. His research focused on the first moments in the lives of various marine animals, such as sandworms, sand dollars, and sea urchins. He became an expert in understanding and explaining how their eggs are fertilized and how these different marine animals develop.

Just longed to devote more time to research, but his heavy teaching load at Howard prevented that. In the mornings, he taught classes to medical, dental, and pharmacy students. In the afternoons, he instructed zoology students.

TIME FOR RESEARCH

Thanks to the support of a benefactor named Julius Rosenwald, Just was able to devote more time to scientific research and less time to teaching. Rosenwald was concerned that an accomplished scientist like Just was being denied access to the well-equipped and staffed research labs at public and private universities that were available only to whites.

Throughout the 1920s and 1930s, a series of grants enabled Just to spend as much as six months a year doing research. The grants also allowed Just to travel to some of the major European centers of research. From 1912 to 1920, Just had only been able to produce nine published papers. But from 1921 to 1930, he wrote thirty-eight papers and made significant contributions to a book on cytology (the study of the biology of cells).

By 1929, Ernest Just was convinced that moving to Europe would advance his career. His work was well-known and well respected by the

A profile image of Ernest Just. ▶

scientists there. Just was better known in Europe than he was in the United States because there was a greater interest among European scientists in his research.

Just had also become increasingly estranged from Howard University. In 1928, he had gotten Rosenwald to award Howard University an eighty-thousand-dollar grant, but little of the money went for new lab equipment or for increased lab space and support staff. Just found that his supervisors had little interest in, or understanding of, his research. He would later write that "I have always felt out of place at Howard."[2] Just would also call Howard "a make-believe university."[3]

In 1930, Just severed his ties with Howard University and the MBL. He became a visiting professor at the Kaiser Wilhelm Institute in Berlin, Germany. The institute had a famous research lab with several Nobel Prize winners on its staff. Ernest Just became not only the first African American but the first American to be invited there.

Just greatly enjoyed his time at the institute. He would later tell some of his MBL colleagues: "I have received more in the way of fraternity

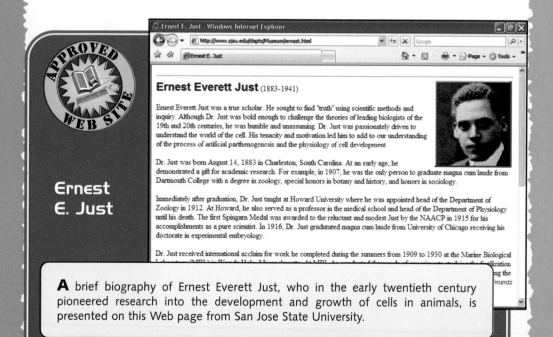

Ernest
E. Just

Ernest Everett Just (1883-1941)

Ernest Everett Just was a true scholar. He sought to find "truth" using scientific methods and inquiry. Although Dr. Just was bold enough to challenge the theories of leading biologists of the 19th and 20th centuries, he was humble and unassuming. Dr. Just was passionately driven to understand the world of the cell. His tenacity and motivation led him to add to our understanding of the process of artificial parthenogenesis and the physiology of cell development.

Dr. Just was born August 14, 1883 in Charleston, South Carolina. At an early age, he demonstrated a gift for academic research. For example, in 1907, he was the only person to graduate magna cum laude from Dartmouth College with a degree in zoology, special honors in botany and history, and honors in sociology.

Immediately after graduation, Dr. Just taught at Howard University where he was appointed head of the Department of Zoology in 1912. At Howard, he also served as a professor in the medical school and head of the Department of Physiology until his death. The first Spingarn Medal was awarded to the reluctant and modest Just by the NAACP in 1915 for his accomplishments as a pure scientist. In 1916, Dr. Just graduated magna cum laude from University of Chicago receiving his doctorate in experimental embryology.

Dr. Just received international acclaim for work he completed during the summers from 1909 to 1930 at the Marine Biological

A brief biography of Ernest Everett Just, who in the early twentieth century pioneered research into the development and growth of cells in animals, is presented on this Web page from San Jose State University.

Access this Web site from http://www.myreportlinks.com

and assistance in my one year at the Kaiser Wilhelm Institute than in all my other years at Woods Hole put together."[4]

IN A TIME OF WAR

Unfortunately, moving to Europe did not revitalize his career. During the 1930s, bleak economic conditions made grants a lot harder to come by. Just was never able to get a long-term research grant. After the Nazis took control of the German government in 1933, Just was forced to leave the country. In 1938, he took up permanent residence in France. During that time, he published his most important work, *The Biology of Cell Surface*. When France fell to the Nazis in 1940, Just was forced to flee again. For a brief time he was held captive in a prisoner-of-war camp.

Since America was not at war with Germany at that time, U.S. State Department officials were able to free Just. Short of funds and unemployed, Just was forced to return to Howard. Just applied for retirement funds from the university, but his claim was denied by its executive committee. Ernest Just died of cancer on October 27, 1941.

IN A TIME OF RACISM

Today, Just is mostly remembered for establishing the important role that the protoplasm and

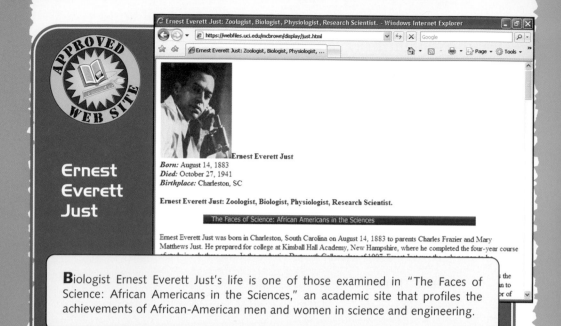

Ernest Everett Just: Zoologist, Biologist, Physiologist, Research Scientist. - Windows Internet Explorer

https://webfiles.uci.edu/mcbrown/display/just.html

Google

Ernest Everett Just: Zoologist, Biologist, Physiologist, ...

Page   Tools

Ernest Everett Just

Born: August 14, 1883
Died: October 27, 1941
Birthplace: Charleston, SC

Ernest Everett Just: Zoologist, Biologist, Physiologist, Research Scientist.

The Faces of Science: African Americans in the Sciences

Ernest Everett Just was born in Charleston, South Carolina on August 14, 1883 to parents Charles Frazier and Mary Matthews Just. He prepared for college at Kimball Hall Academy, New Hampshire, where he completed the four-year course

Ernest Everett Just

Biologist Ernest Everett Just's life is one of those examined in "The Faces of Science: African Americans in the Sciences," an academic site that profiles the achievements of African-American men and women in science and engineering.

Access this Web site from http://www.myreportlinks.com

the ectoplasm play in the cell development of marine animals. Prior to his research findings, it was believed that all the activities of the cell were controlled by the nucleus. Just concluded that the protoplasm (the substance living outside the nucleus) and the ectoplasm (the outer layer of the protoplasm) both greatly influence the activity of the nucleus during fertilization and determining gene heredity.

Just had the misfortune of living in a time when racism denied him the opportunities to pursue his research full time and live out his dreams of scientific achievement. The National Academy of Sciences often consulted Just on membership selections, but it never allowed him to become a member. In spite of his impressive résumé, Ernest Just was never offered a job at a major research institution.

Just would even discourage African-American students from seeking science careers. He would advise them to go into other fields like medicine, where he believed that African Americans would have a greater chance of succeeding.

In the journal *Science,* writer Frank Lillie summed up Ernest Just's career by noting: "Just's scientific career was a constant struggle for research, the breath of his life. An element of tragedy ran through all Just's scientific career due to the limitations imposed by being a Negro in America, to which he could make no lasting psychological adjustment despite earnest efforts on his part."[5]

Walter E. Massey

Taking a test that he had not signed up for led Walter Massey to a college scholarship and then on to an outstanding career as an educator, researcher, administrator, and physicist.

In 1953, Walter was fifteen years old when his schoolteacher mother asked him to go with her to drive some of her students from Hattiesburg to Jackson, Mississippi. The students were all high-achieving

Lifeline

1958: Receives BS in physics from Morehouse College.

1970: Joins faculty Brown University a co-founds Inner-C Teachers of Science

1938: Born in Hattiesburg, Mississippi, on April 5.

1966: Receives PhD in physics from Washington University.

high-school students taking tests to earn college scholarships from the Ford Foundation. The foundation was giving scholarships to pay college expenses for the best and brightest African-American students from Mississippi and other southern states.

As the test takers assembled in a large classroom, Walter Massey and his mother waited outside the room. Some testing officials noticed that Walter did not have anything to do, so they invited him to take the test. Since he was not expecting to be tested, he was not nervous or overly concerned about how he did. Later, he would learn that he had the best score of all the students from Mississippi. Walter Massey's

1979: Becomes director of Argonne National Laboratory.

1975: Change *magazine* names him one of America's one hundred most important educators.

1987: Elected president of the American Association for the Advancement of Science.

outstanding performance earned him a Ford Foundation scholarship to Morehouse College in Atlanta. He was admitted there when he was only sixteen.

🧪 GROWING UP DURING SEGREGATION

Walter Massey was born in Hattiesburg, Mississippi, on April 5, 1938. His father, Almar, was a steelworker and his mother, Essie, was a teacher. Walter's parents always encouraged him and his younger brother to work hard in school and stay out of trouble.

In the 1950s, blacks and whites did not attend the same public schools in Mississippi and other

AAAS:
History
and
Archives

In 1989, physicist Walter E. Massey became the first African American to preside over the American Association for the Advancement of Science. Learn more about the AAAS from its archives.

Access this Web site from http://www.myreportlinks.com

southern states under a policy known as segregation. Despite attending segregated schools, Massey said that he had many outstanding teachers.

"The South really had a remarkable class of black professional people," Massey said. "Because they couldn't get jobs elsewhere, they went into teaching. So the schools were bad but the teachers were really very inspirational and knowledgeable, and they would instill the right kinds of attitudes and habits."[1]

When he entered Morehouse College, Walter Massey had the intelligence, but the not the academic background for doing college level work. Although he would later major in physics, Massey had not even heard of the subject when he started college. His high school had not offered classes in chemistry and physics.

Massey credits a Morehouse professor, Dr. Hans Christiansen, with keeping him in college. Dr. Christiansen provided Massey with one-on-one tutoring. He let Massey know that he was not going to accept failure or quitting. In 1958, Massey received his BS in physics from Morehouse. The teen student who wanted to give up had become an honors graduate.

▲ Walter Massey became a renowned scientist through his work with liquid helium. But it was his dedication to teaching science in the inner city for which he may be most well-known today.

🧪 GRADUATE STUDIES

Massey knew he would have to earn advanced degrees before he could become a professional physicist. Since he was only twenty years old, he decided to take some time off before continuing his education. He spent the next two years teaching—one year at Morehouse and then one year at Howard University in Washington, D.C.

By age twenty-two, Massey was ready to go back to school. With the help of Dr. Christiansen, Massey was accepted into graduate school at Washington University in St. Louis, Missouri. He entered graduate school with a confident attitude, but that changed after his first math exam.

Massey thought that he had breezed through the test. He thought that the questions were easy and he finished the test early. When the tests were handed back, Massey was stunned to find that he missed ninety-one of the one hundred questions. Once more, discouragement set in, but again Massey found a mentor to help him. This time, Eugene Feenberg, a theoretical physicist, helped him with his studies.

"If he [Feenberg] had not taken extraordinary care," Massey told a writer from the *Scientific American,* "I would have quit."[2] Thanks to Feenberg's help, Massey received both his MA and PhD degrees from Washington University in 1966.

🧪 WORK WITH HELIUM

Massey's first position as a professional physicist was working at the Argonne National Laboratory in Batavia, Illinois. Some of his research focused on the new field of cryogenics, the study of materials kept at very low temperatures. His main research was concerned with the effects of very low temperatures on helium.

Helium is an odorless, colorless, tasteless gas. It normally occurs as a lighter-than-air gas. Yet, it shows some special properties at extremely low temperatures. The gas will not liquefy until temperatures are only a few degrees above absolute zero (−460 degrees Fahrenheit). It is the only chemical element that will not freeze by simply cooling. As the gas cools and liquefies, it also must be compressed, or packed together, like when making a snowball. When helium does liquefy, it becomes what is known as a superfluid that leaks through the glass walls of a container. Liquid helium is very useful as a coolant during research on the flow of electricity. Unlike most other liquids, liquid helium manages heat extremely well. It flows toward relatively warmer places, and it also expands instead of contracts when it cools.

Massey's research on liquid helium earned him a promotion to staff physicist at Argonne. Massey enjoyed his research and he found it fulfilling because he was judged on the quality of his work and not on his race.

"I went into theoretical physics because I wanted something I could do by myself," Massey explained. ". . . When you're black and you grow up segregated, so much depends on how people think of you. In theoretical physics, no one reading one of your papers would know if you were

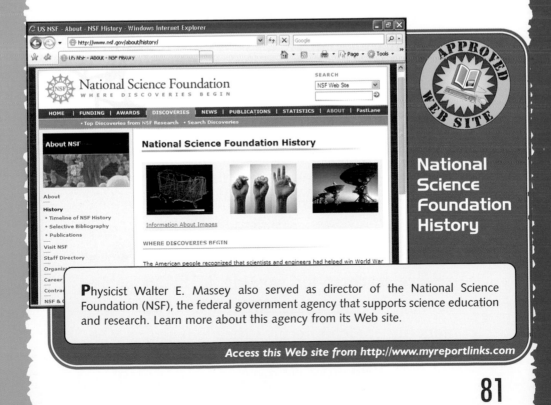

National Science Foundation History

Physicist Walter E. Massey also served as director of the National Science Foundation (NSF), the federal government agency that supports science education and research. Learn more about this agency from its Web site.

Access this Web site from http://www.myreportlinks.com

black or white. There's no such thing as black physics."[3]

🧪 Helping Others

Still, Massey had a nagging feeling that his scientific research was not doing much to help other African Americans. He left Argonne to become an assistant professor at the University of Illinois (UI). During his first year there, the university began an affirmative-action program to recruit more African-American students. Massey became concerned that the African-American students entering UI were not academically prepared for college level work.

"The problem was that the [black] students who came did not have the necessary preparation in high school, and they could not make it up at the college level," Massey said. "That's when I got interested in pre-college science education."[4]

Massey began attacking that problem after he joined the faculty at Brown University in 1970. He started a program called Inner-City Teachers of Science. Massey's program trained science teachers for working in urban public schools where most African-American and minority students receive their education. The program also developed teaching activities for public-school science programs. All the while, Massey still managed to teach classes and conduct research on why liquid helium muffles sound waves passing through it.

A MAN OF IMPORTANCE

In 1975, Brown University promoted Massey to the rank of professor. That same year, *Change: The Magazine of Higher Learning* listed Massey as one of America's one hundred most important educators. Massey's research and administrative skills were attracting the attention of other universities. In 1979, Massey was lured back to the Argonne National Laboratory. He became its director, while also teaching physics at the University of Chicago.

Since then, Massey has gone on to receive many other honors. In 1987, he was elected president of America's largest science organization, the American Association for the Advancement of Science (AAAS). Four years later, President George H. W. Bush appointed Massey the director of the National Science Foundation (NSF).

The NSF is the federal government's leading scientific agency. As its director, Massey was responsible for overseeing an annual budget of more than 2 billion dollars and for awarding

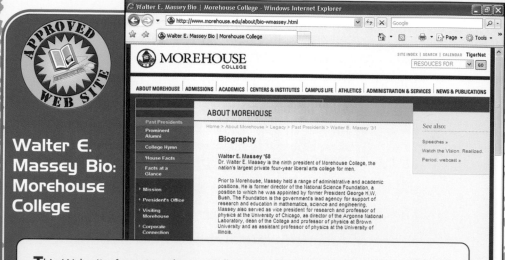

APPROVED WEB SITE

Walter E. Massey Bio: Morehouse College

Walter E. Massey Bio | Morehouse College - Windows Internet Explorer

http://www.morehouse.edu/about/bio-wmassey.html

Walter E. Massey Bio | Morehouse College

MOREHOUSE COLLEGE

SITE INDEX | SEARCH | CALENDAR TigerNet

RESOUCES FOR

ABOUT MOREHOUSE | ADMISSIONS | ACADEMICS | CENTERS & INSTITUTES | CAMPUS LIFE | ATHLETICS | ADMINISTRATION & SERVICES | NEWS & PUBLICATIONS

Past Presidents
Prominent Alumni
College Hymn
House Facts
Facts at a Glance
> Mission
> President's Office
> Visiting Morehouse
> Corporate Connection

ABOUT MOREHOUSE

Home > About Morehouse > Legacy > Past Presidents > Walter E. Massey '31

Biography

Walter E. Massey '58
Dr. Walter E. Massey is the ninth president of Morehouse College, the nation's largest private four-year liberal arts college for men.

Prior to Morehouse, Massey held a range of administrative and academic positions. He is former director of the National Science Foundation, a position to which he was appointed by former President George H.W. Bush. The Foundation is the government's lead agency for support of research and education in mathematics, science and engineering. Massey also served as vice president for research and professor of physics at the University of Chicago, as director of the Argonne National Laboratory, dean of the College and professor of physics at Brown University and as assistant professor of physics at the University of Illinois.

See also:
Speeches »
Watch the Vision Realized.
Period: webcast »

This Web site from Morehouse College includes a biography of Dr. Walter E. Massey, distinguished African-American scientist, who served as the college's president from 1995 to 2007.

Access this Web site from http://www.myreportlinks.com

thousands of grants for scientific, mathematical, and technological research.

🧪 HIS LASTING DEDICATION

From 1995 until 2007, Walter Massey served as the president of his alma mater, Morehouse College. Prior to that, he had served as the senior vice president of academic affairs and provost (high-ranking university administrative official) of California's massive state university system. Returning to Morehouse enabled Massey to return to teaching and encourage minority students to pursue science careers.

"At this point in my career, I wanted to get back to an environment where I have more direct contacts with students and faculty," Massey said. "I've been involved in programs around the country, at the national level, to try to promote more opportunities for minorities in science and to encourage minority youngsters to pursue science, and I decided that I should go back and get more involved at a grassroots level."[5]

John P. Moon

If you have ever used the "save" command on a computer, you have utilized some of the technology that computer scientist John P. Moon helped to develop and refine. Before the Zip drive became widely used and readily available in the early

Dr. John P. Moon

Lifeline

1938: Born in Philadelphia, Pennsylvania, on July 15.

1958: Receives BS in mechanical engineering from Penn State University.

Chapter 7

1990s, Moon helped to develop the floppy disks that preceded their use.

John P. Moon was born in Philadelphia on July 15, 1938. His father, Perry, was a construction worker who would patiently answer his curious son's questions about how things worked. When his father did not have the answers, John would look for the answers himself. He would spend hours building model planes and cars or taking apart old radios and other electronic devices.

In high school, John's favorite subjects were science, mathematics, and English. After graduating from high school with high honors, he enrolled at Pennsylvania State University to study engineering. He graduated with a BA in mechanical engineering in 1960.

1964: Receives MS in mechanical engineering from New York University.

1990s: Developed diskettes for Apple's Mac computers.

1962: Hired by IBM.

1970: Employed by the National Micronetics Corporation.

🧪 WORKING WITH *IBM*

In the early 1960s, International Business Machines (IBM) was one of the world's leaders in manufacturing, selling, and servicing business computers. At that time, IBM was making a special effort to diversify their workforce by recruiting and hiring African-American scientists and engineers. They hired Moon in 1962, even though he lacked a background in computer science.

"I'm self-taught, basically," Moon would later admit. "I had to work at this."[1]

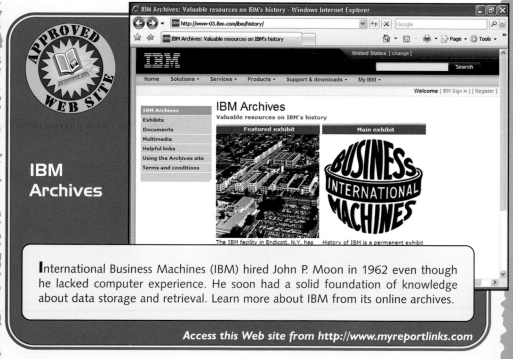

IBM Archives

International Business Machines (IBM) hired John P. Moon in 1962 even though he lacked computer experience. He soon had a solid foundation of knowledge about data storage and retrieval. Learn more about IBM from its online archives.

Access this Web site from http://www.myreportlinks.com

When Moon started at IBM, laptop and desktop computers did not exist. The computers built by IBM were huge, expensive mainframe machines that would fill an entire room. Only a few large corporations used these early computers.

Moon began working at a time when IBM was looking for improved methods of storing and retrieving data. IBM's computers used heads, which read data from magnetic tape and floppy disks, that were a combination of metal and ferrite (a magnetic substance). The heads were manufactured by a high-temperature process that caused the metal and ferrite to bond.

Moon worked with a team of IBM employees to adapt existing methods from other industries for improved manufacture of the heads. His work put him in contact with chemists, physicists, and engineers. He began to acquire a solid foundation of knowledge about data storage and retrieval. The more he learned, the more he wanted to learn.

"You find out you don't know, and you're bound to learn," Moon said. "It just grew over time. Achievement in one part of the business led to another part . . . then I'd work at that, and then get into another part, and so on."[2]

🧪 PERFECT TIMING

Moon left IBM in 1970 after they asked him to move from New York to California. He joined a new company called the National Micronetics Corporation (NMC). They knew about Moon's experiences in working with ferrite disk heads. They made him the company's engineering director.

He joined the right company at the right time. Moon and his colleagues at NMC began manufacturing the heads when there was a rapidly expanding market for their product. In just a few years, NMC grew from a few employees working out of a garage to a multi-million-dollar company.

Around 1974, NMC bought out a small southern California company that made a specialized kind of disk drive. Several years after telling IBM he did not want to move to California, Moon found himself moving to San Diego. He became part of the management team that took over the operations of NMC's new acquisition.

Moon enjoyed his work and his new home, but he began to feel that NMC did not offer enough opportunities for advancing his career. In 1976, he began working for the Tandon Magnetics Corporation (TMC).

⚗ SATISFYING MARKET DEMAND

TMC had been founded by "Jugi" Tandon. By the mid-1970s, the first microcomputers, or personal computers, were being manufactured and sold. These newer computers used small transistors and silicon microchips instead of the big, bulky radio tubes found in the large mainframe computers. As they became more widely used, consumers wanted a way to save and store more data than the computer's memory could hold.

The first floppy disks only stored data on one side of the disk. They were not able to store much data. Tandon solved that problem by

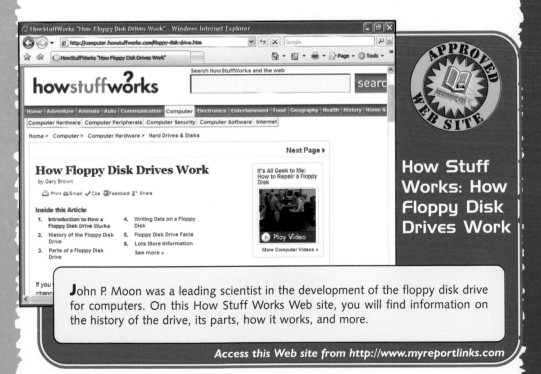

How Stuff Works: How Floppy Disk Drives Work

John P. Moon was a leading scientist in the development of the floppy disk drive for computers. On this How Stuff Works Web site, you will find information on the history of the drive, its parts, how it works, and more.

Access this Web site from http://www.myreportlinks.com

91

▲ John Moon is best known for helping improve the 3.5 inch floppy disk (center.) This image shows various computer storage devices that people have used over the past thirty years.

inventing a double-sided disk head that could store and retrieve data on both sides of a disk. Now a disk could hold twice as much data. In a short time, there was a great demand for his invention.

Moon helped TMC meet the skyrocketing demand for their product by finding a way to mass-produce the disks. TMC experienced tremendous growth and began making hard and floppy disk drives as well as disk heads. Moon's success at TMC attracted the attention of Apple Computers.

A "SELF-TAUGHT" IN CHARGE

John Moon did not want to leave TMC, but Rod Holt, Apple's chief scientist, kept contacting and pursuing him. For a while, Moon refused to even speak to Holt, but Holt would not give up. One Saturday morning, Holt caught Moon in his office at TMC. After they talked, Moon agreed to meet and talk with some executives at Apple.

Moon was favorably impressed with the people at Apple, but he did not want to leave San Diego. Apple's headquarters was located in Cupertino, California, which was more than four hundred miles northwest of San Diego. Holt and Apple wanted Moon so badly that they asked him where he wanted to live.

When Moon told them he wanted to stay in San Diego, they agreed to set up a disk head plant in that area. After they found a suitable location in Thousand Oaks, California, Moon left TMC to work for Apple. "It was an opportunity to do my own thing, so I took it," Moon said.[3]

Moon supervised the plant in Thousand Oaks for four years. During that time, he helped to design and produce several new floppy and hard disk drive heads. His most important achievement was to make improvements in the design and storage capacity of the three-and-a-half-inch floppy disk.

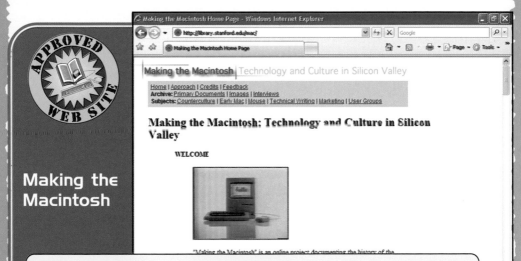

Making the Macintosh

One of John P. Moon's most important achievements working for Apple, makers of the Macintosh computer, was in improving the design and storage capacity of its three-and-a-half inch disks. This site from Stanford University offers a history of the Macintosh.

Access this Web site from http://www.myreportlinks.com

🧪 A HUMBLE EXAMPLE OF INSPIRATION

Although he has been an innovator, John Moon modestly says that his inventions have not been responsible for any major changes in the computer industry. He merely acknowledges that he has been around some things that have changed the industry. He also acknowledges that some people have disliked him because of his race, but he never let that hold him back.

"I'm sure there were some people that didn't like me because I was black, or who questioned my ability because of that," Moon said.[4]

Moon believes that the most important thing for young people of any race seeking a science career is to find something they really like and want to work at. In short, something that makes them feel, "Gosh, this is interesting, I want to do this and learn more about it. That leads to being good at it. Be good at what you do, and don't let people's attitudes slow you down."[5]

Daniel Hale Williams

Daniel Hale Williams was a true pioneer in the education and training of African-American doctors and nurses and in innovative surgical techniques. In his most famous operation, he risked his reputation to save a human life. The landmark operation is regarded as one of the first successful heart surgeries in medical history.

🜂 EARLY YEARS

Daniel Williams was born in Hollidaysburg, Pennsylvania, on January 18, 1856. His father,

Lifeline

1883: Receives medical degree from Chicago Medical College.

1893: Performe first recorded successful heart surgery.

1856: Born in Hollidaysburg, Pennsylvania, on January 18.

1891: Provident Hospital opens.

Chapter

Daniel, Sr., was a barber and his mother, Sara, was a homemaker. He was the fifth of seven children. Some accounts say that both of Williams's parents were African American, while other accounts say that they were of mixed African-American, American Indian, and white ancestry.

Williams was sometimes mistaken for being white since he had a light complexion, blue eyes, and red hair. There is no evidence that Williams ever tried to pretend that he was not an African American. By all accounts, he was always proud of his ancestry and who he was.

Daniel, Sr., died when Williams was only eleven. Sara was unable to support all seven children by herself. She was forced to break

1897: Returns to Provident Hospital.

2004: Northwestern University dedicates an auditorium and atrium in his honor.

1894: Pres. Cleveland names him surgeon in chief of Freedmen's Hospital.

1931: Died in Idlewild, Michigan, on August 4.

up her family by sending the children to boarding schools or to live with relatives.

When the family split up, Williams became an apprentice to a shoemaker who was a friend of the family. He did not care for that line of work and he soon quit his position. For a few years, Williams traveled and supported himself by doing odd jobs. Eventually, he settled in Janesville, Wisconsin, with an older sister. Williams took up his father's trade and became a barber.

⚗ ASSISTANT TO THE DOCTOR

While working as a barber, Williams became friends with Henry Palmer, a local doctor. Dr. Palmer was impressed with Williams's intelligence and dexterity of his hands. He hired Williams as an assistant. In later nineteenth century America, it was a common practice for aspiring doctors to work with an experienced doctor before attending medical school.

Dr. Palmer taught Williams some of the basics of medicine—setting broken bones, delivering babies, stitching up wounds, and diagnosing and treating common illnesses. After two years of assisting Dr. Palmer, Williams was accepted to attend the Chicago Medical College. Today, that college is part of Northwestern University.

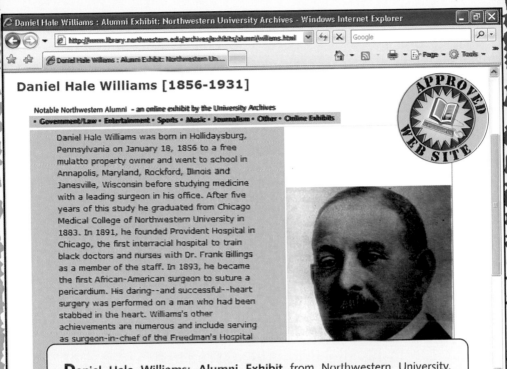

Daniel Hale Williams [1856-1931]

Notable Northwestern Alumni - an online exhibit by the University Archives
• Government/Law • Entertainment • Sports • Music • Journalism • Other • Online Exhibits

Daniel Hale Williams was born in Hollidaysburg, Pennsylvania on January 18, 1856 to a free mulatto property owner and went to school in Annapolis, Maryland, Rockford, Illinois and Janesville, Wisconsin before studying medicine with a leading surgeon in his office. After five years of this study he graduated from Chicago Medical College of Northwestern University in 1883. In 1891, he founded Provident Hospital in Chicago, the first interracial hospital to train black doctors and nurses with Dr. Frank Billings as a member of the staff. In 1893, he became the first African-American surgeon to suture a pericardium. His daring--and successful--heart surgery was performed on a man who had been stabbed in the heart. Williams's other achievements are numerous and include serving as surgeon-in-chief of the Freedman's Hospital

Daniel **Hale Williams: Alumni Exhibit** from Northwestern University, provides a biography of notable alumnus Daniel Hale Williams. In 1891, Dr. Williams became the first surgeon to perform a successful heart operation.

Williams began his studies in 1880 and received his medical degree three years later.

🧪 *DOCTOR DAN AND PROVIDENT HOSPITAL*

In medical school, Williams had shown a talent for surgery. It became his specialty when he opened his private practice in Chicago. He soon earned a reputation for being both a caring doctor and a skilled surgeon. His patients fondly called him Doctor Dan and kept his practice thriving.

Williams's work was greatly influenced by the English surgeon, Joseph Lister, and the French microbiologist, Louis Pasteur. Lister was famous for discovering that a surgeon's hands, medical instruments, and surgical dressings had to be germfree to prevent the spread of infection. His techniques practically eliminated the problem of postsurgical infections.

Pasteur is noted for discovering that diseases are caused by germs multiplying inside the body. Pasteur is also credited with developing medicines called vaccines that prevent the spread of diseases in animals and humans.

In his practice, Williams treated patients of all races. It bothered him to see how difficult it was for African Americans to get into medical and nursing schools. At that time, it was a common practice to reject prospective students just on the basis of race. He decided to start a hospital that treated people of all races and that would also serve as a nursing school for African-American women and offer internships to African-American doctors.

Williams solicited funds from some wealthy businessmen, such as railroad sleeping-car manufacturer George Pullman and meat-packing magnate, Philip D. Armour. He held fund-raisers and persuaded friends to donate money to the

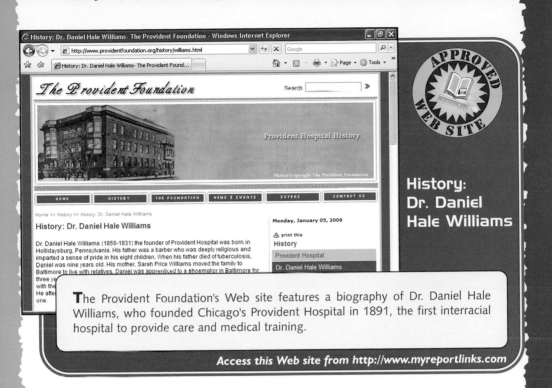

The Provident Foundation. Provident Hospital History.
Photos Copyright The Provident Foundation.

HOME   HISTORY   THE FOUNDATION   NEWS & EVENTS   EXTRAS   CONTACT US

Home >> History >> History: Dr. Daniel Hale Williams

History: Dr. Daniel Hale Williams

Dr. Daniel Hale Williams (1856-1931) the founder of Provident Hospital was born in Hollidaysburg, Pennsylvania. His father was a barber who was deeply religious and imparted a sense of pride in his eight children. When his father died of tuberculosis, Daniel was nine years old. His mother, Sarah Price Williams moved the family to Baltimore to live with relatives. Daniel was apprenticed to a shoemaker in Baltimore for three ye...

Monday, January 05, 2009

🖨 print this
History

Provident Hospital
Dr. Daniel Hale Williams

The Provident Foundation's Web site features a biography of Dr. Daniel Hale Williams, who founded Chicago's Provident Hospital in 1891, the first interracial hospital to provide care and medical training.

Access this Web site from http://www.myreportlinks.com

History:
Dr. Daniel
Hale Williams

hospital. In 1891 the twelve-bed Provident Hospital opened. Williams now had a hospital where he could perform operations. At that time, African-American doctors were barred from performing surgeries in Chicago's other hospitals.

🧪 SURGERY

At Provident Hospital, Williams performed his most famous operation. In July 1893 a man named James Cornish was admitted to Provident after being stabbed in the chest. At first, it looked like a minor wound, but Williams

Provident Hospital and
Training School for Nurses,
Chicago.

▲ The Provident Hospital building in Chicago. Dr. Daniel Hale Williams is pictured in the inset on the upper left and two nurses who graduated from the school are pictured in the inset on the right.

noticed that Cornish was rapidly weakening. Williams observed that the wound was in the left side of the chest. He deduced that Cornish was suffering from internal bleeding in the area around his heart.

At that time, there were no X-rays, sonograms, or CAT scans to allow doctors to locate and diagnose internal injuries and bleeding. Blood transfusions were not used then. Williams knew that he had to act quickly to save Cornish's life. He decided that he needed to operate.

After slicing through skin and cartilage, Williams saw that the point of a knife blade had nicked a blood vessel. The pericardium, a membrane surrounding the heart, had also been damaged. Williams stopped the bleeding by tying off the blood vessel. Then, Williams sewed up the wound in the pericardium. Cornish made a full recovery and went on to live for another twenty years.

A MASTER SURGEON AND EXAMPLE

News of the operation made Williams a well-known surgeon. In 1894, President Grover Cleveland appointed Williams as the surgeon in chief at the Freedmen's Hospital in Washington, D.C. The hospital had been established after the

Civil War to provide medical care for freed slaves.

Williams's work there enhanced his reputation as both a surgeon and as a hospital administrator. Under his leadership, the hospital was reorganized and became staffed by both African-American and white doctors. A nursing school similar to the one at Provident Hospital was also organized. The hospital's death rate dropped and its reputation as a quality health-care facility improved.

While working at Freedmen's, Williams also helped found the National Medical Association (NMA). The NMA enabled African-American

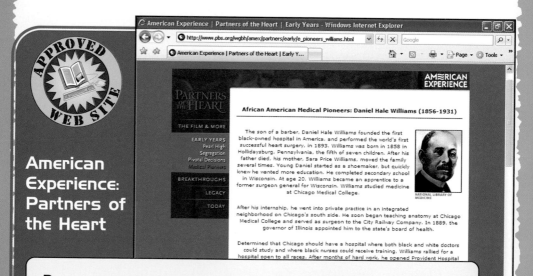

American Experience: Partners of the Heart

African American Medical Pioneers: Daniel Hale Williams (1856-1931)

The son of a barber, Daniel Hale Williams founded the first black-owned hospital in America. and performed the world's first successful heart surgery, in 1893. Williams was born in 1858 in Hollidaysburg, Pennsylvania, the fifth of seven children. After his father died, his mother, Sara Price Williams, moved the family several times. Young Daniel started as a shoemaker, but quickly knew he wanted more education. He completed secondary school in Wisconsin. At age 20, Williams became an apprentice to a former surgeon general for Wisconsin. Williams studied medicine at Chicago Medical College.

After his internship, he went into private practice in an integrated neighborhood on Chicago's south side. He soon began teaching anatomy at Chicago Medical College and served as surgeon to the City Railway Company. In 1889, the governor of Illinois appointed him to the state's board of health.

Determined that Chicago should have a hospital where both black and white doctors could study and where black nurses could receive training. Williams rallied for a hospital open to all races. After months of hard work, he opened Provident Hospital

Partners of the Heart, a PBS site, focuses on a medical collaboration between doctors of different races made possible by the sacrifices of Dr. Daniel Hale Williams, pioneering African-American surgeon, and others like him.

Access this Web site from http://www.myreportlinks.com

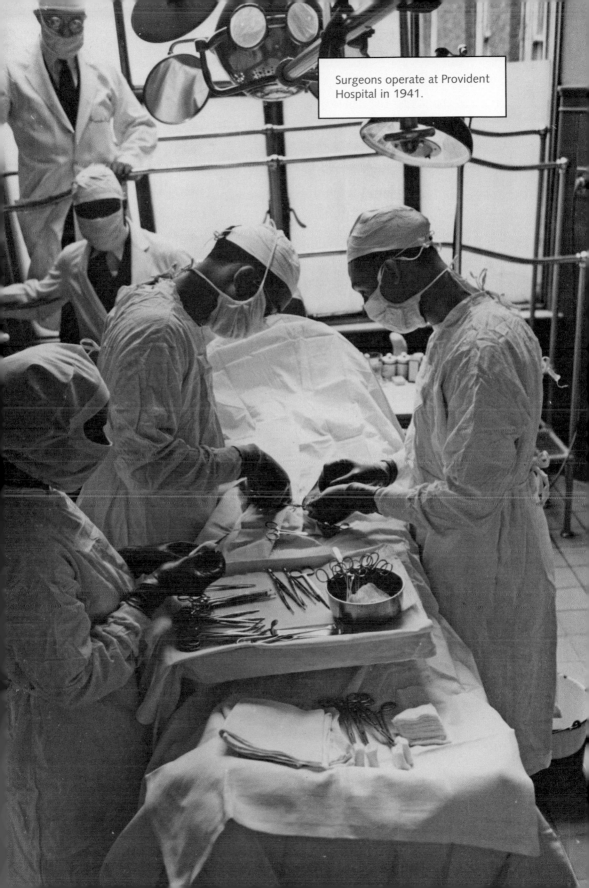

Surgeons operate at Provident Hospital in 1941.

doctors to network and share their knowledge and expertise with their colleagues. At that time, membership in the American Medical Association (AMA) was closed to African-American doctors.

Williams returned to Provident Hospital in 1897. He continued his work as a surgeon and administrator. He also traveled as a visiting professor at medical schools and as an adviser for establishing hospitals to serve African-American communities. During his career, he helped establish forty hospitals in twenty states. Williams passed away on August 4, 1931.

Today, Daniel Hale Williams is remembered for his successful work in improving the quality of medical care for African Americans and increasing the availability of educational opportunities for African Americans pursuing medical careers. Still, much of his work aided people of all races. Williams believed that quality health care and job opportunities in medicine should be available to people regardless of their race.

In 2004, Northwestern University honored Williams by dedicating an auditorium and atrium in his honor. During the dedication, Dr. Lewis Landsberg, dean and vice president for medical affairs at the university's medical school, summed up Williams's outstanding life and career by saying:

Dr. Dan was a master surgeon, a wonderful teacher, and in many ways one of the most accomplished leaders in American medicine at the turn of the twentieth century. He was a leader in the broadest sense of the word. He brought real change for the better for the people he interacted with. He set a lasting example for many others.[1]

Jane Cooke Wright

Cancer is usually a fatal disease. There is still no known cure. But, thanks to the dedicated research of Dr. Jane Cooke Wright, lives of cancer victims have been prolonged and sometimes saved.

Jane Wright was born in New York City on November 30, 1919. Her father, Dr. Louis Tompkins Wright, was

Lifeline

1942: Receives BA in premed from Smith College.

1952: Becomes head of Harlem Hospital's Cancer Research Foundation after the death of her father.

1919: Born in New York City, New York, on November 30.

1945: Earns medical degree from New York Medical College.

an eminent surgeon, a cancer researcher, and a leader in the civil rights movement. Her father was one of the first African Americans to graduate from Harvard Medical School. He was also a well-respected surgeon at Harlem Hospital, the first African American on the staff. Her paternal grandfather and a step-grandfather were both prominent physicians. Her only sibling, Barbara, is also a physician.

🧪 CHOOSING A CAREER PATH

Jane Wright originally planned on becoming an artist. After graduating from Fieldston, an exclusive private high school in New York City, Wright won a four-year scholarship to study art at Smith College in Northampton, Massachusetts. At the start of her junior year, Wright changed her major to premed. Her father had convinced

1971: First woman elected president of the New York Cancer Society.

1967: Becomes associate dean at New York Medical College, the highest ranked African-American woman at a nationally recognized medical school.

1987: Retires from practicing medicine.

her that it would be difficult to make a living as an artist.

Wright's academic record at Smith won her a four-year scholarship to New York Medical College. In medical school, she was vice president of her class and president of the honor society. Wright graduated third in a class of ninety-five and received her MD with honors in 1945.

For the next year, Wright interned at Bellevue Hospital in New York City. During her internship, her supervisor rated her as "by all odds the

Changing the Face of Medicine | Dr. Jane Cooke Wright - Windows Internet Explorer

http://www.nlm.nih.gov/changingthefaceofmedicine/physicians/biography_33

Google

Changing the Face of Medicine || Dr.. Jane Cooke Wright

Page Tools

* BIOGRAPHY   Return

Dr. Jane Cooke Wright

YEAR OF BIRTH / DEATH	
b. 1919	
MEDICAL SCHOOL	
New York Medical College	
GEOGRAPHY	
LOCATION	New York
PATH	
Teaching	
Oncology	

Changing the Face of Medicine: Dr. Jane Cooke Wright is part of a Web site of the National Library of Medicine that focuses on the contributions of women. This page presents a brief biography of pioneering cancer researcher Dr. Jane Cooke Wright.

most promising intern I have ever had working for me."[1]

🧪 CANCER RESEARCH AND TREATMENT

After completing a two-year residency at Harlem Hospital, Wright decided to specialize in internal medicine. For a few months, she worked as a visiting physician at Harlem Hospital. Then, she became a clinician at the hospital's Cancer Research Foundation, which had been established by her father.

The foundation staff concentrated on the effects of drugs on tumors and other abnormal growths. Their work also focused on the use of chemotherapy in treating cancer. After her father died in 1952, Wright succeeded him as the foundation's director.

Wright found her new position challenging and fulfilling. Chemotherapy and the development of anticancer drugs were relatively new fields and Wright found herself at the forefront of research and discovery in those areas.

"There's lots of fun in exploring the unknown. There's no greater thrill than in having an experiment turn out in such a way that you make a positive contribution," Wright said.[2]

Then, as now, the major difficulty in developing anticancer drugs is finding drugs that attack

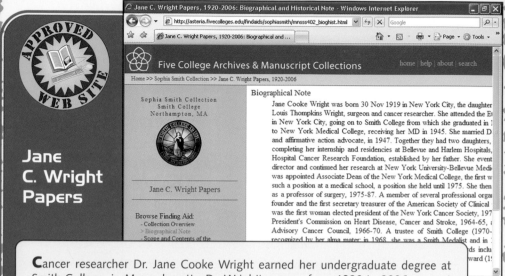

Cancer researcher Dr. Jane Cooke Wright earned her undergraduate degree at Smith College, in Massachusetts. Dr. Wright's papers from 1920 to 2006 are part of the college's Sophia Smith Collection.

Access this Web site from http://www.myreportlinks.com

and kill cancer cells without causing harmful side effects. Most anticancer drugs are also toxic to normal cells. Cancer cells do not differ greatly from normal cells. Finding a drug that kills cancer cells without harming normal cells has been a great challenge.

PROMISE WITH UNCERTAINTY

One of Wright's most promising discoveries was a drug called mithramycin. It is closely related to the antibiotic streptomycin. In one study during the 1960s, Wright found it was useful in fighting a type of brain cancer that was deeply embedded in the brain.

Wright and her team of researchers tested the drug on a group of fourteen patients who were near death. Eight of the fourteen showed improvement. Three of those eight appeared to have been cured, but with all cancer patients there is a risk the cancer will return later.

One of the many difficulties faced by cancer researchers has been that different forms of cancer respond to the same anticancer drug in different ways. Another problem is that different patients will respond to the same drug in different ways. Doctors have had great difficulty in selecting the treatment that best matches the specifics of a certain cancer with the unique reactions of a patient.

Dr. Wright worked on solving that problem by removing a few cancer cells from the patient's body. Usually, the removed cells will multiply under controlled laboratory conditions. After the cells have formed a colony, they can be treated with a cancer-fighting drug. If the drug does not work on the lab-grown cells, then it will not work inside the patient's body.

A DIFFICULT LINE OF WORK

Wright's research and experiments have helped to eliminate the practice of using ineffective drugs to fight cancer. Like all scientists and

113

researchers, Wright has had to cope with failure and frustration. Yet, she never gave up.

"Chemotherapy can be depressing . . . and I must say there are many failures," Wright admitted. "But I have seen tumors vanish. . . . With the right drugs cures are possible."[3]

During her career as a cancer researcher, Wright's biggest discouragement was the lack of funding for finding a cure for cancer. In an interview in the late 1960s, she told one reporter:

> The money made available for cancer research by the federal government amounts to some one hundred seventy-six million dollars a year. Contrast this to the five hundred fifty-three million dollars spent in this country for greeting cards, or the three hundred fifty-eight million dollars for chewing gum. If we can afford these things, why can't we put enough money and enough people to work to solve the cancer problem?[4]

A Dedicated Doctor

Before her retirement in 1987, Wright made many significant contributions. She found techniques for injecting anticancer drugs directly into the cancerous growth instead of a nearby vein or artery. Wright is also credited for developing ways of rerouting the arteries that feed the location of the cancer. By doing that, the anticancer drug goes only to the cancer site and

▲ *Dr. Wright is perhaps best known for a technique called polychemotherapy, in which chemotherapy and prescription drugs are used in tandem to fight cancer.*

APPROVED WEB SITE

Jane Cooke Wright Biography

Jane Cook Wright Biography - Windows Internet Explorer

http://www.aacr.org/home/scientists/scientific-achievement-awards/micr-wrig

Google

Jane Cook Wright Biography

Page ▾ Tools ▾

American Association for Cancer Research

Home | Centennial | About Us | Scientists | Survivors & Advocates | Public & Media | Membership

SCIENTISTS

about this image

Font Size: a a a   Send to a Colleague ✉   Search   GO   Advanced Search   Quick Links

Home > Scientists > Scientific Achievement Awards > MICR Wright Lectureship > Jane Cooke Wright Biography

SCIENTISTS

Distinguished Lectureship in Breast Cancer Research

Outstanding Investigator Award

Lifetime Achievement Award

Landon Prizes

Pezcoller-AACR

Jane Cooke Wright Biography

The AACR-Minorities in Cancer Research-Jane Cooke Wright Lectureship, sponsored by the AACR-Minorities in Cancer Research, is named in honor of **Jane Cooke Wright, M.D.**, a pioneer in clinical cancer chemotherapy and an exceptional scientist who is African-American and who has made important contributions to research in this field.

Dr. Wright made her mark in cancer research analyzing a wide range of anti-cancer agents, exploring the relationship between patient and tissue culture response, and developing new techniques for administering cancer chemotherapy. She was among the

As a cancer researcher, Dr. Jane Cooke Wright helped to develop many of the drugs used to fight cancer today. This Web page of the American Association for Cancer Research, which has named a lecture series in her honor, provides a biography of Dr. Wright.

Access this Web site from http://www.myreportlinks.com

it does not spread throughout the patient's body. That practice had reduced hair loss and other negative side effects in cancer patients.

Before retiring, Wright did important work and research in the practice of using combinations of drugs along with chemotherapy for fighting cancer. This is known as polychemotherapy. Using drugs in combination with chemotherapy causes cancer cells to be attacked by several means at the same time. Cancer cells are deprived of nutrients and also prevented from reproducing.

Although cancer remains a disease without a cure, the anticancer drugs that Wright has helped to test and develop have saved or pro-longed countless lives. Dr. Jane Cooke Wright's dedicated and unselfish work has inspired future generations of doctors, researchers, and scientists to find a cure for this deadly disease.

Report Links

The Internet sites described below can be accessed at
http://www.myreportlinks.com

▶**The Faces of Science: African Americans in the Sciences**
Editor's Choice Learn about other African Americans who have made contributions in science.

▶**Science Update: Spotlight on African-American Scientists**
Editor's Choice Learn about some of the leading African-American scientists working today.

▶**African-American Innovators**
Editor's Choice A site for teachers lists some of the scientific contributions of African Americans.

▶**National Museum of African American History and Culture**
Editor's Choice Learn about African-American history and culture through a new museum Web site.

▶**Mathematician and Astronomer Benjamin Banneker**
Editor's Choice This Library of Congress site features three pages on the life of Benjamin Banneker.

▶**RPI: Profile of Shirley Ann Jackson**
Editor's Choice Rensselaer Polytechnic Institute's Web site offers this biography.

▶**AAAS: History and Archives**
Browse the archives of the AAAS, once headed by Walter E. Massey.

▶**Africans in America: Benjamin Banneker**
A PBS site on African-American history looks at the life of Benjamin Banneker.

▶**American Experience: Partners of the Heart**
A PBS site looks at African American medical pioneers.

▶**American Red Cross Museum: Dr. Charles Drew**
Read about Dr. Charles Drew's lifesaving work with the American Red Cross during World War II.

▶**Changing the Face of Medicine: Dr. Jane Cooke Wright**
Dr. Jane Cooke Wright is celebrated on this site from the National Library of Medicine.

▶**Daniel Hale Williams: Alumni Exhibit**
The Northwestern University archives offer a biography of distinguished alumnus Daniel Hale Williams.

▶**Ernest E. Just**
A university site looks at the life of Ernest Everett Just, pioneering biologist.

▶**Ernest Everett Just**
A brief online biography of this legendary scientist.

▶**George R. Carruthers: Physicist of the African Diaspora**
A university site presents a brief biography of astrophysicist George Carruthers.

Report Links

The Internet sites described below can be accessed at
http://www.myreportlinks.com

▶**History: Dr. Daniel Hale Williams**
A biography of Dr. Daniel Hale Williams, the founder of Provident Hospital, is featured.

▶**How Stuff Works: How Floppy Disk Drives Work**
Learn about the floppy disk drive and how it works.

▶**IBM Archives**
Learn more about IBM, where John P. Moon first worked with computers.

▶**Inventor of the Week: Charles Richard Drew**
At this site, learn about the African-American physician who originated the concept of blood banks.

▶**Inventor of the Week: George Carruthers**
Learn more about the life and career of astrophysicist George Carruthers from this MIT site.

▶**Jane C. Wright Papers**
Read a brief biography of Jane Cooke Wright on this college Web site.

▶**Jane Cooke Wright Biography**
A cancer research organization looks at the life of pioneering researcher Dr. Jane Cooke Wright.

▶**Lemelson Center Invention Features: George Carruthers**
Astrophysicist George Carruthers is profiled in this Smithsonian site.

▶**Making the Macintosh**
This site draws on Stanford University archives to offer a history of the Macintosh computer.

▶**National Science Foundation History**
Find out more about the National Science Foundation, once headed by Walter E. Massey.

▶**NSF.gov News: Shirley Ann Jackson**
Dr. Shirley Ann Jackson received an award recognizing her contributions to scientific research.

▶**Red Gold: Innovators and Pioneers: Charles Drew**
A PBS Web site examining the "epic story of blood" presents this biography of Dr. Charles Drew.

▶*Time Magazine:* **Benjamin Banneker**
A magazine article examines Benjamin Banneker's challenge to Thomas Jefferson.

▶**Unsung Heroes: Ernest Everett Just**
A *Time Magazine* site honors Ernest Everett Just as a forgotten hero of science.

▶**Walter E. Massey Bio: Morehouse College**
Learn about Walter E. Massey's tenure as the ninth president of Morehouse College.

Glossary

alma mater—A school where one has studied.

atom—The smallest unit of an element.

CAT scan—An X-ray picture of a cross section of the body.

clinician—A person qualified in the clinical practice of medicine, psychology, or psychiatry.

cytology—The branch of biology dealing with the function, structure, and life history of cells.

cytoplasm—The substance between the membrane and the nucleus of a cell.

ectoplasm—The outer portion of a cell's cytoplasm.

ephemeris—A chart that shows the positions of the moon, sun, and planets for every day of the year.

gristmill—A mill used for grinding grain.

humanitarian—A person concerned with helping to improve the lives of other people.

liquefy—To make or become a liquid.

molecule—A group of two or more atoms linked together by sharing electrons.

nucleus—The positively charged central portion of an atom.

nutrient—A substance that furnishes nourishment.

paradigm—The accepted way of looking at an issue.

plasma—The liquid in which blood cells float.

platelets—Tiny flat particles found in blood that help the blood to form clots.

protoplasm—The contents of a living cell.

provost—A high-ranking college official.

red blood cells—The blood cells that receive oxygen from the lungs and carry it to the rest of the body.

sonogram—A visual image produced from ultrasound waves penetrating the body.

thesis—A research paper prepared by a student seeking to earn an advanced college degree.

toxic—Something poisonous.

tumor—An abnormal cell growth.

ultraviolet light—Electromagnetic radiation with wavelengths shorter than visible light, but longer than X-rays.

white blood cells—The blood cells that fight off infections.

Chapter Notes

Introduction

1. Colin A. Palmer, editor in chief, *Encyclopedia of African-American Culture and History* (Farmington Hills, Mich.: Thomson Gale, 2006), vol. 5, p. 2,020.

Chapter 1. Benjamin Banneker

1. Ray Spangenburg and Kit Moser, *African Americans in Science, Math and Invention* (New York: Facts On File, Inc., 2003), p. 8.

Chapter 2. George R. Carruthers

1. James H. Kessler, J. S. Kidd, Renee A. Kidd, and Katherine A. Morin, *Distinguished African-American Scientists of the Twentieth Century* (Phoenix: Oryx Press, 1996), p. 39.

2. "HALL OF FAME/ inventor profile," *Invent Now*, n.d., <http://www.invent.org/hall_of_fame/185.html> (February 27, 2007).

Chapter 3. Charles R. Drew

1. Spencie Love, *One Blood: The Death and Resurrection of Charles R. Drew* (Chapel Hill: The University of North Carolina Press, 1996), p. 109.

2. Charles E. Wynes, *Charles Richard Drew: The Man and the Myth* (Urbana: University of Illinois Press, 1988), pp. 18–19.

3. Jessie Carney Smith, ed., *Notable Black American Men* (Detroit: Gale Research Inc., 1999), p. 332.

4. Douglas Starr, *Blood: An Epic History of Medicine and Commerce* (New York: Alfred Knopf, 1998), p. 100.

Chapter 4. Shirley Ann Jackson

1. "Aim for the Stars," *Rensselaer.MAG*, September 1999, <www.rpi.edu/dept/NewsComm/Magazine/sept99/jackson_1.html> (February 27, 2007).

2. Willie Ginn, "Shirley Ann Jackson," *Current Biography Yearbook 1999* (New York: H. W. Wilson & Company, 1999), p. 284.

3. Joannie M. Schrof, "Her Brilliant Career," *ASEE Prism Online,* n.d., <www.prism-magazine.org/nov99> (February 27, 2007).

4. "The Three-Legged Stool," *Rensselaer.MAG,* September 1999, <www.rpi.edu/dept/NewsComm/Magazine/Sept99/jackson_3.html> (February 27, 2007).

5. Ginn, p. 284.

6. Ibid., p. 285.

Chapter 5. Ernest Everett Just

1. Ray Spangenburg and Kit Moser, *African Americans in Science, Math and Invention* (New York: Facts On File, Inc., 2003), p. 139.

2. Lisa Yount, *Black Scientists* (New York: Facts On File, Inc., 1991), p. 33.

3. Ibid.

4. Ibid., p. 35.

5. Ibid., p. 142.

Chapter 6. Walter E. Massey

1. Elizabeth A. Schick, ed., *Current Biography Yearbook: 1997* (New York: H. W. Wilson and Company, 1997), p. 357.

2. Emily J. McMurray, ed., *Notable Twentieth-Century Scientists* (Detroit: Gale Research, Inc., 1995), p. 1,326.

3. Schick, p. 358.

4. Ibid.

5. Ibid., p. 359.

Chapter 7. John P. Moon

1. Lisa Yount, *Black Scientists* (New York: Facts On File, Inc., 1991), p. 96.

2. Ibid., p. 97.

3. Ibid., p. 101.

4. Ibid., p. 103.

5. Ibid.

Chapter 8. Daniel Hale Williams

1. Zondra Hughes, "Northwestern University honors the legacy of 'Dr. Dan': America's first open heart surgeon," *Ebony,* December 2004, p. 78.

Chapter 9. Jane Cooke Wright

1. Jean Elder Cazort, *Notable Black American Women* (Detroit: Gale Research Inc., 1992), p. 1,284.

2. Charles Moritz, ed., *Current Biography Yearbook 1968* (New York: H. W. Wilson Company, 1968), p. 444.

3. Ibid.

4. Ibid., p. 445.

Further Reading

Cox, Clinton. *African American Healers.* New York: Wiley, 2000.

Cullen, Katherine. *Marine Science: The People Behind the Science.* New York: Chelsea House, 2006.

Jones, Lynda. *Five Brilliant Scientists.* New York: Scholastic, 2000.

Moser, Kit, and Ray Sangenburg. *African Americans in Science, Math, and Invention.* New York: Facts On File, 2003.

O'Connell, Diane. *Strong Force: The Story of Physicist Shirley Ann Jackson.* New York: Franklin Watts, 2004.

Schraff, Anne. *Dr. Charles Drew: Blood Bank Innovator.* Berkeley Heights, N.J.: Enslow Publishers, 2003.

Sullivan, Otha Richard. *African American Women Scientists and Inventors.* New York: Wiley, 2002.

Venezia, Mike. *Charles Drew: Doctor Who Got the World Pumped Up to Donate Blood.* New York: Children's Press, 2009

Weatherly, Myra. *Benjamin Banneker: American Scientific Pioneer.* Minneapolis, Minn.: Compass Point Books, 2006.

Index

A

abolition, 6
affirmative action, 82
American Association for the Advancement of Science, 83
American Astronomical Society, 35
American Indians, 97
American Medical Association, 106
American Red Cross Blood Bank, 45
Amherst College, 37
ancient Greece, 14
ancient Rome, 14
Apollo 16, 27, 32
Apple Computers, 93–94
Argonne National Laboratory, 80–81, 83
Armour, Philip D., 100
astronomy, 10, 18–19, 24, 25, 30
Atlanta, Ga., 76

B

Baltimore, Md., 11, 39
"Banked Blood: A Study of Blood Preservation," 42
Bannaka, 12
Banneker, Benjamin, 5, 10–21, 51
Banneker, Mary, 12
Banneker, Robert, 12, 16
Batavia, Ill., 80
Bell Telephone Laboratories, 59
Bellevue Hospital, 110
Benjamin Banneker's Pennsylvania, Delaware, Maryland and Virginia Almanack and Ephemerris, 19
Berlin, Germany, 70
Bethune, Mary McLeod, 51
Bible, 16
The Biology of Cell Surface, 71
Black Engineer of the Year Award, 35

Black Issues in Higher Education, 62
Black Student Union, 58
Blood for Britain, 44
Boston City Hospital, 58
Bouchet, Edward Alexander, 6
Britain, Great, 44–45
Brown University, 58, 82–83
Buck Rogers, 23
Bush, George H. W., 83

C

Cambridge, Mass., 55
cancer, 108, 111–114, 116–117
Cancer Research Foundation, 111
Carruthers, George R., 9, 22–35
Carruthers, George R., Sr., 22–23, 24
Carruthers, Sophia, 24
Change: The Magazine of Higher Learning, 83
Charleston, S.C., 64
chemotherapy, 111, 114
Chicago, Ill., 24–25, 99, 101
Chicago Medical College, 98
Chicago Planetarium, 25
Christiansen, Dr. Hans, 77, 79
Cincinnati, Ohio, 22
Civil War, 103
Cleveland, Grover, 103
Clinton, Bill, 60
Collison, Michele, 62
Colonial America, 5, 15
Colored Normal Industrial, Agricultural, and Mechanical College, 65
Columbia University Medical School, 41
computer technology, 9, 86–91
Cornish, James, 101, 103
Cupertino, Calif., 93
cytology, 68

D

Dartmouth College, 66–67
Drew, Charles R., 6, 36–49
Drew, Nora, 36–37
Drew, Richard T., 36–37
Dunbar, Paul Laurence, 51

E
Ellicott, Andrew, 16
Ellicott, George, 16, 18
Ellicott, John, 16
England, 11
Englewood High School, 24–25
European Center for Nuclear
Research (CERN), 59
Exceptional Achievement
Scientific Award, 35

F
Feenberg, Eugene, 79
Fermi National Accelerator
Laboratory, 58
Fieldston School, 109
Ford Foundation, 58, 75–76
Ford, John R., 47–48
France, 71
Freedmen's Hospital, 47,
103, 104

G
Germany, 44, 71

H
Hall, Jacob, 13–14
Hanover, New Hampshire, 66
Harlem Hospital, 111
Harvard University, 39, 58, 109
Hattiesburg, Miss., 74, 76
heart surgery, 103
Hollidaysburg, Pa., 96
Holt, Rod, 93
Howard University, 39, 41, 47,
67–70, 71, 79

I
IBM, 88–89
influenza epidemic, 39
Inner-City Teachers of Science,
82–83

J
Jackson, Beatrice, 51
Jackson, George, 51
Jackson, Miss., 74
Jackson, Shirley Ann, 50–63
Janesville, Wis., 98
Jefferson, Thomas, 19, 21
Just, Charles, 65
Just, Ernest Everett, 6, 64–73

Just, Mary, 65

K
Kaiser Wilhelm Institute, 70–71
Kimball Union Academy, 66

L
Landsberg, Dr. Lewis, 106
Lillie, Frank, 73
Lister, Joseph, 100

M
Marine Biological Laboratory
(MBL),
67, 70
marine biology, 64, 67
Massachusetts Institute of
Technology (MIT),
55, 58
Massey, Almar, 76
Massey, Essie, 76
Massey, Walter E., 6, 74–85
mathematics, 10, 13
McGill University, 39–41
mechanical engineering, 87
medicine, study of, 38, 41, 96,
104, 106
mithramycin, 112
Montreal, Canada, 39
Montreal General
Hospital, 41
Moon, John P., 9, 86–95
Moon, Perry, 87
Morehouse College, 76, 77, 79,
84
Morgan State College, 39
Museum of Science and
Industry, 25

N
NASA, 33
National Academy of Sciences,
72–73
NAACP, 47
National Board of Medical
Examiners, 41
National Institutes of Health, 49
National Medical Association
(NMA), 104, 106
National Micronetics
Corporation (NMC), 90

National Science Foundation, 58, 83–84
National Technical Association, 33
Nazis, 71
New Jersey Commission on Science and Technology, 59–60
New York City, 108, 110
New York Medical College, 110
Nobel Prize, 70
Northampton, Mass., 109
Northwestern University, 98–99, 106
Nuclear Regulatory Commission (NRC), 60, 62

O
Orangeburg, S.C., 65
ozone layer, 32

P
Palmer, Henry, 98
Pasteur, Louis, 100
Paul Laurence Dunbar High School, 37
Pennsylvania State University, 87
Philadelphia, Pa., 87
physics, 49, 58, 77, 79–80, 82
plasma, 36, 42, 44–45
polychemotherapy, 116
Provident Hospital, 101, 104, 106
Pullman, George, 100

Q
Quakers, 12

R
racism, 6–7, 10, 45, 47, 71–73
Rensselaer Polytechnic Institute (RPI), 62
Rosenwald, Julius, 68–69
Rutgers University, 59

S
San Diego, Calif., 90, 93
Science, 73
Scientific American, 79
segregation, 77
slavery, 6, 10, 12, 19, 21, 103

Smith College, 109
Society of Friends, 12
South Carolina State University, 65
space travel, 9, 27, 30, 32–33
Spingarn Medal, 47
St. Louis, Mo., 79

T
Tandon, "Jugi," 91
Tandon Magnetics Corporation (TMC), 90–91, 93, 94
Theodore Roosevelt High School, 53–54
Thousand Oaks, Calif., 94
Tuskegee, Ala., 47

U
ultraviolet light, 27
University of Chicago, 58, 67, 83
University of Illinois, 25, 82
U.S. Army, 47
U.S. Civil Rights Bill (1964), 7
U.S. Naval Research Laboratory, 27, 35
U.S. Navy, 25, 47
U.S. Postal Service, 24, 49
U.S. State Department, 71

W
Walsh, Molly, 11–12
Warner Prize, 35
Washington, D.C., 21, 36, 51, 79, 103
Washington, George, 19
Washington University, 79–80
Williams, Daniel Hale, 96–107
Williams, Daniel Hale, Sr., 97
Williams, Sara, 97–98
Woods Hole, Mass., 67, 71
World War II, 36, 39
Wright, Barbara, 109
Wright, Jane Cooke, 108–117
Wright, Louis Tompkins, 108–109

Y
Yale University, 6
Young, John W., 27

Z
zoology, 64, 67, 68